Boo
Fan
Faxi

piring. I doubt whether anyone's life will remain
ed after reading it' *Here's Health*

olin Turner writes is worth reading' *Business Age*

positive results' *Evening Standard*

ommended' *Financial Times*

d\   )aily Mail

k a   d fu   f seriously good advice' *The Irish News*

M
Ne   preaches what he has practised' *Sunday Independent*

O   king person's Little Book of Calm' *Belfast Telegraph*
S

searched yet intuitive' *N. Holloway MD, Microsoft UK*

s West for success' *His Excellency, Ma Zengang*

's philosophy works' *C. Cowdray, CEO, Claridges*

ulsory reading' *Dr Marilyn Orcharton, Founder, Denplan*

excellent blueprint for success' *Sir Michael Grylls*

philosophy for the 21st Century'
a Peiffer, 'Positive Thinking'

meless Wisdom' *Kyodo News*

'A source of inspiration – read it!' *BBC*

service@21stcenturybooks.co.uk

COLIN TURNER

Swimming with Piranha
makes you Hungry

21st
Century
Books

Swimming with Piranha makes you Hungry

Copyright © Colin Turner 1997
Illustrations Richard Pearce

The right of Colin Turner to be identified as the Author of the Work has been asserted by him in accordance with the Copyright, Design and Patents Act 1988

First published in Great Britain in 1998 by Intoto
Published in 1998 by Hodder & Stoughton

This edition Published in Great Britain in 2004 by
21st Century Books UK Ltd
30 Queen Square, Bristol, BS1 4ND

www.21stcenturybooks.uk.com
service@21stcenturybooks.uk.com

Cover Design by Dick Evry, Bath
Printed and bound in the UK by The Bath Press,
Lower Bristol Road, Bath, England

British Library Cataloguing in Publication
Data available

ISBN: 1-904956-05-X

Special Thanks

To the "Fish" who have changed the course of their lives mid-stream and never looked back. To the intrepid Chrissie Krevchenko for finding those Fish. To the illustrious illustrator, Richard Pearce, it is always great fun working with you. To dedicated Dick Evry, a shining light amongst graphic designers. To unflappable Tricia Hawkins whose last minute input was just great. To my wife, Sharon, whose love and support makes all my work worthwhile. And to four very special fish who always swim to the brim: Jason, Dylan, Caleb and Shamira.

Quoted by Time magazine as being a leading
authority on success, business and lifestyle,
Colin Turner's thought-provoking books have been
translated into 30 languages. Combining Eastern philosophy
and contemporary Western experience into practical,
relative and accessible form they include:

Contents

Part One

A Prologue

Part Three

Swimming with Piranha makes you Hungry

Part One

A Prologue

A Prologue

Renowned for their voracity and reputed ferocity, piranha travel in groups and usually prey on other fish. They are attracted to the scent of blood and can reduce even a large animal to a skeleton in a short time. Before Modern Man appeared they enjoyed the top position for consumption.

Although they have a herd instinct when a tasty morsel, or any morsel for that matter, is discovered, it's every piranha for him or herself. They will dive right in at the slightest indication of any deal and take advantage of the situation to grab what they can, not stopping until they reach the bone. Nothing is left in the path of their voracious consumerism. More and more doesn't seem to satisfy them, it doesn't even phase them. Amazingly, it's as if they still remain hungry however bloated they may become.

A happy piranha is one who is in the thick of the action. Only when the water is literally boiling with grabbing whatever it can, does it feel at its most secure. Those times that it finds itself in calm waters do not rest easy with it at all, so, usually it will create the opportunity to pick a fight with a neighbour, particularly if that neighbour appears to have more. After all that wouldn't be fair, would it?

Pete Piranha wondered if it had always been like this. He felt different from the others because something inside told him that life didn't have to be this way. He had been told he was really lucky because the neighbourhood that he lived in had not always had such an abundant food supply. Since the floods of a few generations ago had joined two rivers together every fish said there would be more than enough. But no fish seemed to know exactly what was enough. It was as if the more they had of everything, the more they not only wanted, but the more they complained and bickered.

The abundance and ease of having all they desired, it seemed to him, made every fish even hungrier. It was as if no matter what was available externally to consume, there remained inside every fish an emptiness, almost a hunger for something else. He couldn't quite put his fin on exactly what it was, but he was determined to try and find out, because the more he competed against other piranha to make a comfortable home for his family, the less he seemed to end up with.

The new, bigger set of teeth he had bought was really going to stretch him, and as for all the flipping and flapping up and down the fast currents everyday, well, that was exhausting. But the schools of elite fish that his children wanted to swim with, and his wife's insistence on owning the latest descaler, meant that he had to carry on.

Pete would often think about the great stories he had been told years ago about how it was in the days before the flood. Fish would only consume when they genuinely needed to and the currents made swimming enjoyable. The new fast currents did not exist at that time, yet now they were so jam packed they were almost at a standstill.

Apparently no undercurrents existed either. Imagine that, he thought to himself, yet now they were everywhere. He was certain that they were the cause of so much of the envy and friction that was now part and parcel of herd life. If you didn't conform to swimming in the way that society deemed was correct, then, my goodness, you certainly felt the undercurrents. Those who had tried to do their own thing, even though it had not affected others, experienced the full tide against them.

1   Hook, Line and Sinker

The cost of a thing is the amount of life which is required to be exchanged for it, immediately or in the long run.
H. D. Thoreau

ARE YOU COMFORTABLE with the way you handle your time, money and life? Certainly there seems to be a correlation between the three. Our 24 hour non-stop society has developed its own motto of 'time is money'. Is it? Is this how we view our time? To get as much done, in order to earn as much as we can, to allow us to live in a style that society has deemed is appropriate or ideal. Is it possible that we have been caught on a self-created hook because of what we have been conditioned to believe?

When we have too much time we often feel guilty because we are not using it to the full. When we have too little we either feel frustrated, because we are unable to get everything done, or important, because we are so busy. It has been said that time is money and, in a way, that is true. For example, imagine a bank that credits your account every morning with £1,400 but, regardless of what you choose to do with this money, at the end of each day the bank cancels out whatever you have failed to use. It goes without saying that you would ensure you used the money in an optimum way. Well, every day we have 1,400 minutes. Every night all lost time is written off, there is no overdraft and no balance carried forward. If you fail to use the day's deposits the way you want it is your loss, no one else's.

We can either choose to live in the present on today's deposits and plan our lives so that we have enough time for what is important to us, or, we can spend it all in continually rushing around dealing with the urgent stuff in life that incessantly bombards us, desperately hoping we will make enough money. Can we ever have enough? Isn't it rather that we never have quite enough, regardless of the time and effort we put into our life?

Do you have enough money? Are you able to enjoy your children growing up or have enough time with the person or people that you want to spend time with? Do you enjoy the work that you spend your time doing, thinking and worrying about? Or is it what you do in order to earn enough to be able to consume more, thereby sustaining, and justifying, the earning? Is yours a life of frantic earning and spending, making more just to consume more?

We have been conditioned to believe that the success of our lives is best measured by the economic gain made during it. So we go for it. Yet as expectations have a habit of rapidly rising to meet, even overtake, their incomes, many people are broke, regardless of how high that income is. And debt is an unforgiving enemy that will immediately appear at the first opportunity provided, such as the disappearance or reduction of earnings.

Have we swallowed hook, line and sinker the belief that only by increasing your standard of living will you increase your quality of life, or, that you must put in more hours to be successful?

Money used to be viewed as a means to an end, but it is now pervasive. We are part of a society that has successfully developed a mechanism that persuades, convinces and even insists that we spend more. Money and acquiring more of it has become a major part of human existence in our country under the misguided belief that more brings security. Are the weary shoppers that emerge from the 'boiling water' of the shopping centre, weighed down with bags of stuff, feeling happier and more secure?

"PHEW! THE THINGS WE DO TO FEEL MORE SECURE"

Perhaps for a short time the excitement of the purchase, made attainable by the credit-card, will bring this, but how high will the level of security be when the statement arrives? Are we in control of our lives or have the hundreds of thousands of adverts we are exposed to every year insidiously become our master? There is no doubt that we do live in a significant period of time. Perhaps now more than any other time in history people are becoming more aware of the influences they are being exposed to. Increasingly there is a conscious awareness of that which is now viewed as perhaps a mindless consumerism.

This awareness is in turn generating a feeling towards having a greater simplicity in life ~ a more natural quality of life not based on having to make sacrifices in relationships with family, friends or community in exchange for career advancement. Not having to defer hopes, ideals and compromise values in the name of making a living and not to be at the beck, call or whim of all those labelled goods which are considered the accepted talisman of success, security and happiness.

The acquisition of what is continually available to us is probably more exhausting than satisfying, as we are not entirely sure whether what we have is what we wanted in the first place. Certainly whenever the latest acquired product is scrutinised it is rarely found to be essential or needed. Moreover, it is soon disposed of or simply discarded.

A NEW WAY OF SWIMMING

Perhaps driven in part by the disillusionment of the heady 1980s and in part by the massive reorganisation of UK business, many are increasingly waking up to the fact that job security is no longer a reality of life. More than any other thing people want some meaning and purpose to their life and it often takes a catalyst to change general perceptions as to what is really wanted, or is possible to achieve and become. The recession was a necessary and valuable pruning time as it began to bring about a change in priorities and values. Very few, after all, were unaffected.

People have begun to ask if they should channel all their energy, strengths, talents and skills into an organisational market-place that views them as merely a commodity. As this is leading from a desire to be in control of their own life, to be more self-reliant and to be in command of their time it is only natural that an alternative is to be sought.

This alternative of living a simpler life with deeper meaning, more time for family and enjoyment, while reducing attachment to status symbols, fast-track careers and an ego enhancing life-style is an increasing attraction. This proven, workable alternative improves the quality of life because it is in line with natural principles. Does the river take the path of the greatest or of the least resistance on its journey to the abundant ocean? The answer is obvious as the river always reaches its goal.

FINANCIAL INDEPENDENCE

Attaining the security of Financial Independence is sought by all. And why not? It is healthy to be in charge of your own life with the feeling of being financially independent.

We live in one of the most prosperous countries in the world with enormous resources and opportunity yet incredibly the majority of people retire either totally dependent on sources external to themselves or continually watching the pennies. Regardless of your income, debt or savings, financial independence is actually achievable by all when its fundamental principles are adhered to. Simplifying your life by uncluttering it and getting yourself in order, is a practice that simply encapsulates all the principles. It is not about 'dropping out' or a 'back to the land' movement. It is a 'make the most of wherever you are' movement. It's about being yourself and employing yourself in a fashion that develops all areas of your life and the lives of those you touch, whether they are close to you or part of the community.

This is not a fad or revolution, it is a choice. The trend is certainly on the increase, but it has been in and out of vogue for centuries. It is about deliberately choosing quality living over quantity buying. It may be that this choice is thrust upon many through the hardship of redundancy. More often, though, it is an action that is deliberately taken and planned in advance. When it is, and the right steps are followed, both means and end provide for a truly fulfilling and meaningful life.

This book is about leaving the boiling waters for calmer ones, about improving the quality of your life, time and relationships without lowering your standard of living. Imagine getting up in the morning because you want to and not because you have to. Imagine being able to watch your children grow while doing what you want. Isn't that what life is all about? That is the reality of life, not the illusion that commercialism insists is a happy life. Yet that is what we have allowed ourselves to be conditioned to believe, which is perhaps why, for many, consuming is a substitute for the void they feel in their lives.

Being able to live the way you live, do the work you do and spend time the way you want, because you have consciously and voluntarily chosen to do so, has got to be a positive ambition and way of life. Of course it doesn't and will not suit everyone, but, for those who feel that this is a path worth investigating seriously, this book will provide the right steps to take. This is no wish book. It will show you whether a less consumer driven, uncluttered and simpler life is right for you. It will help you to focus on what 'the good life' means to you, how you can prepare psychologically for the change, what you can expect and, importantly, how you can become financially independent in the process.

KNOWING WHEN ENOUGH IS ENOUGH

"I've had it! Enough's enough. There must be more to life than leaving for work before the kids are up and getting home when they are asleep."

Brian Longtooth worked for the River Bank and he had chosen to commute rather than move yet again. He and his wife Lucy wanted to have some stability for their children who were at a school they liked, it was difficult enough to find a good school, and they had friends. They were having the opportunity to develop roots. Commuting had seemed the best idea, at the time, particularly as Lucy had a good part-time receptionist position which she enjoyed. The realities, however, were different. They enjoyed living just outside Streamdon and did not want to move, but he had had to take the job just south of the estuary or he would not have had one. It was a two hour haul each way.

"It's amazing to think that I allowed myself to put up with it for so long. I never had enough time with my family and the week-ends were a joke. I was so tired. I lacked the enthusiasm to do anything, other than eat, drink and watch TV. It was my way of recharging the batteries I suppose, at least that's what I always used to tell myself, and when the kids asked if we were going to do anything, I'd say that I'd think about it and that's all I did."

Most of the time Brian was thinking how would he cope if he continued the way he did and how would the family cope if he didn't. Even with the low mortgage rate that he received as a River Bank employee there was never quite enough.

Often it is not until the pain of a situation becomes intolerable that our frustration causes us to rant and rave about doing something to change the situation we are in. Too often though we allow our passion to subside and continue to do what we have always done until the next outburst, nervous breakdown or heart attack. When what we do for a living is simply to bring us enough to live, then when and how do we know when enough is enough?

Without some form of definite and reliable measurement how can whatever we do, particularly with regard to how much we earn, and spend, be satisfying? If we believe that having more has got to be better, then, whatever we have, can never be enough. Brian was suffering from not having enough time with his family as well as not having enough money, even though he was sacrificing the former for the latter. His frustration of 'enough is enough' was perhaps a by- product of the first two emotions yet it was this that acted as the catalyst for him to take action. He had to establish some strategy or go crazy. At any one moment we are being controlled or in control but it is not until one establishes some form of measurement for what will fulfil our lives that we are able to become self-reliant.

But what measurement to use? Brian and Lucy's combined earnings were considerably higher than that of both their parents and grandparents put together yet both remember having enough as children despite the fact that there were twice as many of them.

Is it because we lack an internal feeling of what will be fulfilling to us, that we have been persuaded, as an alternative, to measure fulfilment externally? Do we measure our enoughness by what advertising says we should want, by what others already have, or by what someone in 'our' position would have? Only 30 years ago the great majority of households did not have double glazing, central heating, colour televisions, dishwashers, microwaves, food processors, indeed the list of what today are regarded as necessities is endless. And the list of services, superstores and choice similarly is endless.

All this is good. This is progress but a return to a life that many would consider austere and indeed would not even consider being a life, is certainly not being advocated. The point is what have we been sold literally?

However, despite owning more time-saving appliances, machines and gadgets, all of which are thought to constitute a 'really good and better life', our tendency is to still not feel fulfilled with what we have.

Operating under the belief that more means better we tell ourselves: "If I could only get more of this or have more of that then everything would be better", but, under this belief the 'more' can never be enough. So, we go on getting deeper in debt and often deeper in despair as the 'more' that was supposed to make life better can never be enough. Have we been successfully persuaded to sacrifice our natural sense of knowing when enough is enough, for the values of commercialism that cannot afford for us to know such a thing?

THE LURE OF EXPEDIENCY

The answer has to be yes. When we decide we want something we usually want it straightaway. Our tendency is to choose what is fast and easy rather than hard and necessary. The availability of easy credit allows us to have what we want when we want it.

We don't have to wait for something by saving for it first so, if it grabs our attention, we buy it. And it is the lure of expediency that makes it difficult for us to actually understand what is enough to fulfil us.

Consider, for a moment, your spending habits. When you go shopping for a specific item do you always come home with just that item or with a host of other items as well ~ products that you never intended buying but nevertheless attracted you to them?

Iain Fishendon reported how his purchases seem to be made almost unconsciously. Iain thought he was living his dream. A swimmingly self-made millionaire at an early age he refers to the almost insidiousness of moving from trawling for amenities to just the outright landing of luxuries.

"Almost as a measure of what I was able to do, I spent money. Sometimes it was for myself but more often it was because I felt it was expected of me."

Perhaps Iain had been persuaded by the sheer weight of advertising and commercialism he was overly exposed to, but the fact was, he admitted, his priorities were all wrong. His *actions were not driven by any inner feeling of what was or could be fulfilling, they were driven more by an external influence that advocates: more equals better.*

Joy Waters summed up her shopping habits with: "I always seemed to spend more than I earned on more than I actually needed. I was certainly not a shop-a-holic, but, unless I had a specific list, I would always spend more, particularly on the weekly shop, than I had intended."

Is that what happens? Have you ever gone shopping for a specific item and arrived home having bought lots of other products that you had not intended to? Is the plan to secretly build up more clutter to dispose of at car-boot sales in three years' time? If at home or the office just take a moment to look around the room where you are currently reading this book. How much is really useful to you or is it just clutter taking up space in your life?

We tell ourselves that we work to pay the bills, but then we spend more than we make, on more than we need, in order that we can live it up on the weekend. This sends us back to work to earn more money to spend on buying more stuff, which we have persuaded ourselves that we need or must have.

Are we living under the misguided belief that earning more money means fulfilment? Surely fulfilment, that deep sense of satisfaction in life continually yearned for, can only come from being consciously aware of what is enough? And that measurement can only be established through a firm set of purpose, values and priorities.

WHAT'S YOUR LIFE CURRENTLY ABOUT?

Have you ever earned the amount of money that you consider yourself to be worth? If you are unable to answer that question then ask yourself if you know how to calculate what you are worth? If you do not know what you are worth and you carry on the way you always have then you will continue to receive what you always have. Unless you change your expectations about your value your future will continue very much in the way it has always been for you. If you consider that you have never quite earned enough, there is always too much month left at the end of the money, always something unexpected to pay for and, regardless of how many hours you put in, it is almost impossible to save, then why should it change?

The degree to which we take the value of our self-worth, our identity and psychological security from what we do for a living, is in direct proportion to how trapped we are. Our job has become symbolic with how successful we are in society. What we do for a job has become our principal conduit for self-expression. When another asks 'What do you do', that favoured introductory question for getting to know you, how do you feel? Are you proud or embarrassed? Do you answer with a 'I'm only a ...' or 'just at the moment I'm between ...' if you are not matching what you think is expected of you, by you or others? Do you prefer to call yourself an executive assistant rather than a secretary or salesperson? Does a better title increase your status? What we do and what we earn have become the primary symbols of success. Hit the fast current and you have really arrived.

MAKING A LIVING

Yet what is it all about when you boil it down? What does it cost you in terms of your life, time and money? If it is what you want to do above all, then it is worth it whatever sacrifice you make. If, on the other hand, it's just what you do in order to make a living have you considered the real cost in time and money? You get up as soon as the alarm goes off, well maybe after the automatic snooze button has been punched. 'God, is it time to get up already?', you ask. A quick glance out of the window tells you it's raining and you scold yourself mentally for bothering with the snooze button as you know that the traffic is going to be worse than its usual hell.

You hit the day's first obstacle straight after your speedy visit to the bathroom. Nothing to wear. You find something to put on, however, and after a quick slurp of coffee you're out the door. You hit the traffic sooner than you expected, cursing the weather and wishing that you had made yourself have a slice of toast or some cereal after all. Rush hour seems to get longer and longer you think, even with flexitime. Your fight with the traffic feels worse today, nobody seems to know what they are doing or how to drive, probably because they're all glued to their fully charged mobiles. You arrive at work and feel frustrated even before you start as you had forgotten to recharge your mobile and couldn't phone in to say you might be late. At work it doesn't improve. If you didn't have the countless interruptions throughout your day you might be able to catch up and get something done. Throw in a few meetings, phonecalls, an unexpected crisis and a major communication problem with a colleague and suddenly it's time to go home.

You stuff some of the mail and reports in your case misguidedly thinking you'll have time to deal with them. By the time you get past the unexpected road works and broken-down lorry it's later than you would have liked. You collapse onto the sofa and watch a little TV before going to bed. As you get into bed you promise yourself that you will make more of an effort with the family tomorrow, particularly at dinner time and after. They understand though, you say to yourself, after all you're doing all this so you can provide a good enough life-style. You fall asleep and before it seems as if you've only had time to blink, the alarm starts its incessant call to order once more.

Bring on the weekends ~ but they're not much better. What should be pleasure-packed is no more than pressure-packed with everything that needs to be done or fitted in. Again most of the time seems to pass without ever getting any of the things done. Even the outing you promised the family had to be curtailed. Anyway they're all right because they went shopping yesterday and came back with a lot of stuff that seems to excite them. It keeps them happy and quiet, that's the main thing. You're relieved you haven't been laid off yet under the reorganisation or downsizing, as the company calls it. The only trouble is you have to fit in the schedules of the ones who have, as well as your own. There just aren't enough hours in the day. Never mind, you're making a living.

THE WORKING MOTHER

The working mother meets the same difficulties except: Mum has to get up earlier to make packed lunches, find clothes for everyone, make breakfast and keep urging the children to get up so that all are ready to go on time. This Mum manages to achieve all this while getting ready herself. Plans for leaving on time go out of the window as one child can't find his homework, another can't find her shoes or a little treasure that they had been especially keeping to show at school. Amid the panic and tears, Mum usually finds everything so that everybody can leave. With several hours of work already done she now arrives at work to start her work.

Regardless of what she does her day will follow the demands of any other working person with the confusion of miscommunications, too much paper, too many calls and constant interruptions all which seem to conspire to ruin what might have otherwise been a productive day. Pleased, however, that she has not had to drop everything and fly to pick up one of the children from school, because they have fallen over or are not feeling well, Mum arrives home in time for her third shift. No rest in front of the TV for her, however, as the demands hit her as soon as she walks through the door. No-one can bear to wait an instant until their requirements are met to show, or tell, her something.

At the same time as dealing with them she begins to unpack the groceries she bought during her lunch break. In the rush she had forgotten to buy something and needs to pop down to the shop to get it. After dinner she tries to delegate the tidying up but ends up doing most of it herself as she feels she will expend more energy nagging than she would doing it herself.

In between settling disputes, helping with homework, reading a story and getting the children bathed and put to bed, Mum is supposed to offer some loving, understanding attention to her husband as he has been working all day. After doing a quick load of laundry and ironing a few things so that everybody has something to wear in the morning she gets into bed quietly so as not to wake her partner who is already asleep. Never mind, she thinks, this way we can have enough.

THE REAL COST OF EARNING

So much of our lives are dominated by what we do to earn money that there is little time to have a life. We're sacrificing our lives, our time, our relationships and our sense of joy for more money but it's happening so slowly that we barely notice. The dreams we had of finding meaning and fulfilment through our jobs begin to fade in our striving for more. Stress begins to fill the void they leave behind.

Many books have been written on over-stress because it is the number one ailment in our country today. Modern by-products of it range from irritability to road-rage and from depression to suicide and these conditions are now viewed as a 'normal' part of life. Breakdowns of nerves, relationship, companies and communication are almost always associated with not having enough money. Yet the amazing thing is that despite all the striving to get more and more the majority of people scrape a meagre existence after they retire. We spend our lives earning money and almost always end up with nothing.

THE 'IT'S WHAT EVERYBODY DOES' FACTOR

Why do we do what we do when it is actually taking us away from what we really want? Is it because we have stopped working to become what we are capable of, and now merely work to acquire? The tendency for people to check a nice car's number plate, as they walk past it, to see how new it is, and therefore its monetary value, illustrates how deep rooted our values and priorities in materialism may have become.

The fact that less than 10 per cent of the global population even own a car, let alone have two, doesn't come in to it. It's what our media, advertising, peer group and society has conditioned us to believe is what is required.

The enormous August car sales' figures and corresponding massive rise in finance deals further illustrates that our priorities may be out of line with fundamental values.

Introduced in the 1960s, under pressure from the motor industry to boost low summer sales, it was a coup de grâce as far as the British ego was concerned. It has now got so out of hand, so logistically difficult to cope with, that, at the time of writing, new quarterly registrations are about to be brought in. Perhaps this is another commercial coup de grâce that knows just how to pander to that ego that continually needs to seek better, newer and more, in order to feel secure.

Apart from cars we stretch ourselves to the limit, usually for 25 years, in order to cover mortgage payments. This is viewed as our main security and must be right, after all it's 'what you do', despite the fact that the majority of people in Germany and France, other reasonably successful European countries, rent.

That is not to say that we should not have nice houses, cars and possessions. What is important is to ensure that you are their master not their slave. Whatever you become, do or choose to purchase you must do because you have decided to and the decision fits in with your established mission, values and priorities and *not* because it's what everyone else does.

Moderation of the personal ego is of great importance towards success, quality of life and financial independence, but the 'shoal' ego is just as important. It is the shoal ego that has conditioned you to do what you do because it genuinely believes it is in your best interest. But why should the end result be any different for you if you carry on doing what you are doing now ~ a life seemingly based on growth, but actually based on surviving, until retirement when the state then 'promises' you will have enough to live on because of the contributions you have made? As the young generation, perhaps wisely, and not without cause, suggest: 'Wake up and get a life!'

ALL THAT I HAVE I OWE TO SOMETHING

The only elements of our lives that are sustainable in the long term we owe to a definiteness of purpose made at various points in our lives. Everything in our life we owe to something but the concern is that we have become reliant on the easy availability of credit for most of it. Unfortunately it often takes a real alarm call, such as a minor heart attack, an accident, a redundancy, a loss, a divorce, an illness or a bankruptcy, to make us re-evaluate our lives and think what we really want out of life.

Our ethos of 'more means better' is not fulfilling and certainly not sustainable. Will you regret not having spent more time at work when you are taking your last few breaths? Will you be thinking about all the cars you did or didn't drive? Will you be thinking about how much you have or haven't accumulated? You may be thinking of all the holidays you didn't take ~ at least the ones you promised you would enjoy with your family ~ but other priorities took place. You will most certainly be thinking that you did not spend enough time not only doing what you would really have liked to have done but also with the people that were important to you, that you loved. Regret for things you have done may be tempered with time, but regret for things you have not done is inconsolable.

Isn't it worth really assessing if the fast-current you are in or working towards is what you want? Its attainment may be exciting and seemingly glamorous as you become carried along on its wave, particularly in the short term. In the long term, however, your aims for an impressive and better standard of living may be self-defeating, particularly in respect of your aims for a better quality of life. But do you have what it takes to make the leap, which it is, to get out of the rapids and be in control of your life?

2 ██████ Why Swallow The Bait?

We seldom think of what we have but always of what we lack.
Schopenhauer

SECURITY-ITIS OFTEN HAS A FIRM GRIP over our lives and it takes courage to risk living our dreams, yet living them is an adventure and as such takes drive, determination, hard work and a very clear focus. These qualities you will recognise as central to any success, and may be particularly associated with the life in the fast lane. The big difference, however, is that they are coupled with being more self-reliant and less concerned about what others think; having more balance in life, and listening to common sense universal principles as a way of life.

Most people actually do want out of what is frequently termed the 'rat-race', but what is really the piranha pace, yet they are suspicious of any alternative simply because they have been conditioned to think that way. Perhaps the possible reasons why you may be caught in the rapids and 'avoiding' a simpler lifestyle in calmer waters are that:

- You are concerned about experiencing a reduction in income, particularly as you feel your family is dependent on it for its living standard.

- You believe that your overdraft and debts are currently too high and it would be better to have the security of more equity in your home.

- You simply do not know what you would really like to do and are worried that if you stop doing what you are doing now you'll fall behind everyone else.

- You are not comfortable about leaving the position you have now attained, after so long, which is indicative of your success and status.

- You are afraid of uprooting the family to a different area where they would have to fit into new schools and not know anybody.

- You think that a move might not provide enough cultural or stimulating opportunities or meet educational and religious requirements.

- You consider that where you would like to live and want to do are not compatible.

It must be remembered that it takes all sorts to make a world and you may well be an individual who is in the fast-current, and will continue to stay in it, because you genuinely enjoy the swirls, eddies and undercurrents that go with it. The clues that will confirm whether it is where you have choosen to be could include:

● You can't seem to earn enough income so your main plans for the future are financial.

● You regret not having a degree and may regularly consider wishing you had an MBA but are too busy to get around to taking one.

● You prefer to listen to audio books rather than spend time reading.

● You choose to work late at the office more out of habit than workload.

● You dislike having to spend time doing domestic jobs, shopping or menial tasks and would rather get someone to do them for you.

● You enjoy the glamour, attention, respect and rewards that doing what you do brings.

Living a less frenzied life often takes a strong motivation. Any major change in the way we live our lives does. Getting out of 'boiling' water is not escaping from problems, as problem solving is an essential part of life. It is more a search for purposeful living which by definition generates a greater peace of mind. Perhaps the main motivation is fuelled by a personal desire to be the best one can be and be true to yourself, convictions and values while doing so. There are, however, seven dominant character traits indigenous to those who do choose to start living the life they really want.

THE SEVEN TRAITS OF STRONG SWIMMERS

1. They have consciously evaluated their needs, habits, strengths and talents in order to recognise and define clearly exactly what they want and will be happiest doing.

2. They do not rely on the approval of others and are entirely independent, self-sufficient and self-reliant. As they believe in themselves they are not concerned about what colleagues or neighbours think about them. They make their own decisions and do not do something because it's what everybody is supposed to do. They have confidence in themselves and what they do and are self motivated enough not to require a work environment to achieve what they have determined to do. In this way they take control of their life and do not feel insecure about not being able to provide for themselves or family.

3. They have enormous energy and vitality because their time is spent working at things they enjoy most and have created the environment that is most suited to them. As they love what they do they are good at it so they do not suffer the fatigue, boredom, resentment and stress associated with having to do something not completely in harmony with choice, talent or skill.

4. They are prepared to sacrifice, by going without, rather than 'paying the price', through easy credit, in order that the overall plan of enjoying a good life, peace of mind and the real benefit of financial independence can be enjoyed. They do not choose to go for the 'quick-fix' and enjoy instant gratification as they understand that that practice is not sustainable in the long-term.

5. They always take the initiative knowing that it is the making of their own decisions that will ultimately affect their time, money and life. In choosing to take the initiative they act proactively, rather than reactively, and as such are in control of directing their own destiny.

6. They are persistent, and do not falter at the first obstacle. Rather they seek to gain strength from the overcoming of it knowing that it is indeed obstacles that will develop their creativity and innovation. They understand that it is adversity that has assisted them to recognise the true value of living the way they do. They have already learned that it is only through persistence that you achieve what you do, but, it is only through persisting in what you truly believe that its achievement actually becomes worthwhile.

7. They have established what values are important to them and strive continually to heed them, because they understand that their inner values are the only true measurement of what having enough means in terms of their sense of fulfilment. In developing a personal vision of what they really want in their lives it is easier to practice the principles and code of ethics they have chosen to live by. In

doing this they have merged what is important to them in all their vocational and vacational activities.

Perhaps the above traits lean towards describing a non-conformist. In a way anyone who escapes to something 'different' must be a non-conformist. Society, however, requests, even demands, that we conform to its particular way of thinking. And to what cost do we surrender our opportunity to build our individual character by copying and so being conditioned by society, which acts in the name of its 'knowing best' for the individual? What *you* must do is all that should concern you and not what others might think. So often we dismiss our own excellent ideas, thoughts and dreams, simply because they are our own, and in turn favour the expression of society. And from where does society gain the expression? From a past non-conformist individual who is no longer alive to threaten the status quo.

The most memorable individuals who have ever lived, and who certainly had lasting effects on society were advocates of a simpler life ~ Jesus, Buddha, Gandhi, Mohammed and Lao Tzu to name the most well known. But living simply is not about getting or finding religion. Its precepts may have similar overtones to a more spiritual way of life, because of the fact it involves having more purpose and meaning through a more balanced life, but, if anything, where religion seeks control, spirituality finds release, which is perhaps the escape mankind continues to yearn for. There are two factors, however, which are, without doubt, essential to simplifying your life. They are the principles of being true to yourself and having belief in yourself.

PRINCIPLES TO WHAT YOU WANT TO ACHIEVE

Principles are not invented by Man or fish, as practices are, and they apply in all situations whatever the circumstances. Principles and causes are the same. They are the underlying source from which the consequences in our lives spring. Whatever we create in our life will bring either harmony or turbulence, depending on how strictly the underlying principle involved is adhered to. For example, being responsible for your own actions is a fundamental principle in building character.

We live in a country that is so full of abundance and opportunity that it is not difficult, given the desire, determination and discipline, to make money. What is hard, though, is keeping it. The creation of wealth and financial independence is a result of the knowledge and observance of the principles that have control over it. These principles are immutable since mankind first started earning money. By following the principles strictly it is possible to start on the path towards financial independence regardless of your job, position, status, conditions or circumstances. A sweeping statement but true nonetheless and then only sweeping because many will not choose to learn, observe or even be receptive to how it can happen for them.

It is too easy to blame one's conditions, interest rates, market falls, recessions, depressions, the government and all and sundry. These are all external economic factors that one should be able to ensure have no control over one's life. In the long-term it is not sufficient to just know what you want, to work dedicatedly towards it with focus and to have goal-driven plans. This may get you what you want, but it does not guarantee that you will keep it. If it were the case the majority of people in our country, one of the most affluent in history, would not be struggling to live on pensions, hand-outs or charities from families and organisations as soon as their earning capabilities are permanently or temporarily truncated, through retirement, redundancy, illness or accident.

The average person in the UK will earn in excess of £1 million during the course of their working career. Even on the minimum wage, earnings will exceed £500,000. This puts our country's average earnings in the top 1 per cent of the global population. We are taught that you have to have money to make money, but even with earning more than 99 per cent of the rest of the world's population there is never enough for us to cope on when adversity, difficulties or the unforeseen strikes. Why? Because ridiculously simple financial principles are not adhered to.

At the height of the euphoric 1980s countless financial consultants were available to advise on how best to deal with your money. Amazingly, one in nine of the working population was employed, either directly or indirectly, in providing the other eight out of nine with some form of financial service or product. Many were extremely hardworking and conscientious but, due possibly to more and more directives to increase returns, the emphasis was perhaps more on 'closing the sale' rather than adhering to the principles of wealth essential for financial independence. Although they must exist, it is difficult to find an individual who has genuinely attained financial independence. A financial independence that means you earn even when you don't work, that you have enough for all your outgoing, unforeseen situations and still some left over. It seemed that regardless of the level of their earnings, the priority was for the next commission, as it was necessary to sustain the lifestyle that they had been persuaded, determined, or been programmed, to think that it was necessary to have.

Earlier you were asked if you had ever earned enough. You may have earned considerably more than you do now and, if so, why is there not enough now? More than likely you have continued to earn increasingly more over the years and will continue to do so, but, do you still have to think about how you are going to cover the end of month bills or that little extra you spent on holiday, at Christmas or at the weekend?

It doesn't have to be like that, it shouldn't be like that and will not be like that if the principles in this book are strictly adhered to.

Can you imagine knowing what is enough and only working, for money, when you choose to and with whom you choose, being able to choose your vocation as the vehicle to provide your income and financial independence and have a measurable plan for achieving financial independence? This is what you should have if you follow the instructions faithfully in this book. You also, though, are the common denominator throughout all your life and your choices are the variable factor so it is vitally important that you begin to build the habits necessary to see you through. Achieving financial independence is not about will-power, it is about habit. The habit of applying principles for its attainment. A principle, remember, is an immutable Law, as is the principle, or Law, of Gravity and, as such, is therefore unsympathetic towards ignorance of it. It operates regardless.

THE LAWS REQUIRED FOR FINANCIAL INDEPENDENCE

Many of us can recall the story of Mr Micawber in Dickens' David Copperfield. Sitting in the debtors prison he solemnly advised his visitor, David, 'to take warning by his fate and to observe that if a man had twenty pounds a year income and spent nineteen pounds, nineteen shillings and sixpence, he would be happy, but that if he spent twenty pounds one shilling he would be miserable'. After which he promptly borrowed a shilling off David for port and cheered up. Even though he was aware of some of the wisdom essential for financial independence, he could not bring himself to observe it, despite advocating what he did know. Isn't it almost second nature for us to know what is best for others despite not having put our own house in order first? Yes it is and why? It is because second nature comes from the way we habitually live our lives.

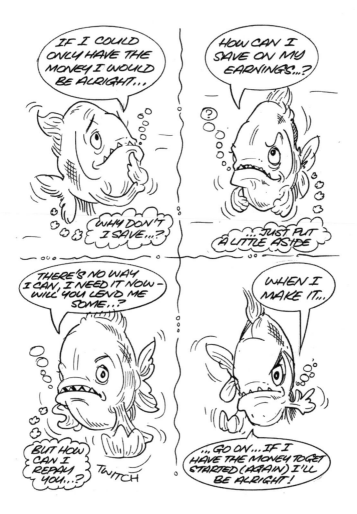

Knowing the laws of financial independence, however, is not sufficient in itself. This is, of course, fundamental to any truth. For example, who is the most ignorant, the person who cannot read or the person who can read, but chooses not to. The only way to adhere to the laws of 'anything' is first to decide whether what you are embarking upon is what you really want for yourself. Secondly, to make a commitment to yourself to stick to your decision. This can only be brought about by developing the habit of personal integrity and this is simply done my making and keeping personal promises.

For this reason each of the seven principles for wealth attainment contained within this book is encapsulated into a promise that you have to undertake to keep before moving on to the next principle. These laws only work when fully applied. If you will undertake to do this then your life will most definitely improve in ways you would never have imagined.

First Law
Promise yourself that, regardless of the amount, you will learn to live on 10 per cent less than you earn.

Second Law
Promise yourself to always save that same 10 per cent you are now learning to live without.

Make the first promise in the knowledge that, regardless of the amount, your income will always unerringly expand to only cover your outgoings until you start to build the dam to your own reservoir. Undertake the second law in the knowledge that the genuine security you seek in your life will indeed come from this 10 per cent saved and not from the 90 per cent spent.

You will undoubtedly and understandably think to yourself that surely this is easier said than done, as the cold reality is that every penny of your earnings is spoken for, or at the very least, committed. The actual reality, however, is that you can and that you must!

What is it that you want most of all? Is it the excitement of regular living purchases such as latest clothes, gadgets, cars, holidays and meals or is to have belongings of substance in the form of land, property, investments that provide income and regular money when you need it. Make no mistake, it is the 90 per cent of your earnings that will bring the first and the 10 per cent that you do not spend that will bring the second.

It is not the amount that you always intend to put by one day, it is not the bonus you are looking forward to, or rather counting on, it is only through strictly following these initial steps that you will be able to guarantee that your plan of financial independence will come to fruition.

Later chapters will show you how you will be able to develop the habit of saving 10 per cent in ways that amazingly will not affect your lifestyle. Those of you who use computers are probably aware that you only use about 10 per cent of its capabilities and each time you learn a simple method you are amazed at how you are able to achieve more in less time cost. The fact is that just because you may not be aware of something does not mean that it does not exist in the same way that just because something sounds so simple does not mean that it cannot be like that. The reality of truth is that it's always simple.

CONSUMPTION

Saving used to be part of our culture but individuals are now viewed as consumers and consumption is believed to be the core ingredient in economic growth. We now believe that it's good and proper to spend, that we have the right to buy and the alternative to not buying is the death of productivity and the economy. Until the last century consumption was the colloquial term for the terminal illness of tuberculosis.

It is strange, but perhaps appropriate, that it is now the cancer of what we really want and indeed our planet can cope with. Perhaps also because the average Britain saves less than 5 per cent of his or her disposable income, each will consume during their life twice as much energy and dispose of twice as much rubbish, which will never be able to be used again, compared with say the Japanese who save 15 per cent of their disposable income.

A baby born in the UK today will have produced about 30 tons of non-recyclable rubbish and used the energy produced of a couple of thousand barrels of oil for their consumption requirements before they have reached the age of 75. To put that in human terms, the equivalent of 300 Ethiopians that also share our planet.

75 YEARS

Just stop reading for a moment and look at your nearest paper or waste bin. Think how often you empty it, just from the junk mail alone, think about what you throw out in a week and what you dump when you get so frustrated you finally have to clear out the garage. The majority of your waste is still unrecyclable, and almost everything that you throw out has just been taking up space in your garage and has cost you money which will have originally come from that 10 per cent that you could not possibly save.

IT STARTS WITH YOU

This is not a book about saving the planet because that can only be a by-product of how individuals choose to live their lives. The interesting paradox though is that there is a direct correlation between financial independence and a better environment. A favourite story of mine is of the bishop who, attempting to write the sermon he wishes to deliver about saving the earth, is prevented from doing so because of the constant interruptions by his young son, who is bored and wants to play.

In his frustration the bishop cuts up a large map of the world into little pieces and says to his son:

"Here go and play with this puzzle of the world. By the time you have put it back together I will have finished my work and will be able to play with you".

Thinking he had at least an hour to finish his sermon the bishop is astonished to see his son back in ten minutes with the excited cry of:

"I've finished that Dad, can we play now?"

"How on earth did you finish it so quickly?", enquired his father looking at his young son.

"It was easy", the boy replied, "on the other side was a picture of a man which I put together knowing that as soon as I got the man put right then the world would be right".

The only way to put our own particular world in order and live the life that will give us the greatest fulfilment is to put ourselves in some sort of order first. You have to start by being as true to yourself as possible in the evaluations of yourself, and what is important to you, as well as for what is asked of you in this book. Unless you know what is 'enough' in your life to enable you to feel fulfilled then it is highly probable that you will never have that feeling, but will always, instead, be wishing things could be better.

If you are frustrated with the commuting, the bickering, other people at work stealing credit for your ideas, the feeling of frustration at making ends meet or at not having what you consider you should have in your position, then the only way things are going to change is for you to change. This means changing your perception of and relationship that you have with money, wealth, security, consuming and the quality of life.

THREE STROKES

In order to perceive the importance of the initial laws encapsulated with: *Regardless of the amount, learn to live on 10 per cent less than you earn and always save that same 10 per cent,* so that it becomes second nature, it is important to do a three-step exercise.

First it is necessary to calculate the nearest approximate amount that you have ever earned in your life. Admittedly this is extremely challenging but the effort is worth it for the end result. There will inevitably be an amount of guestimation in proportion to the period of years that you have been working but it is important to try and include every extra bonus, windfall or gift that came your way.

Only you are going to see this so try and be as honest with yourself as possible. Also include loans, because you have had the use of the money, and winnings ~ in fact the rule is, if in doubt, do not leave out ~ even odd-jobs, paper rounds, part-time work. Looking at bank statements and income tax returns will help. If you find this almost impossible to do, are unable to do it for any reason or indeed are not fully convinced as to the importance of the exercise, then at least make the nearest estimate as possible, for you owe yourself that much effort at least. The main objective is to find out how much money has entered into your life.

Having completed the first stroke you are probably aware, for the first time, how much you have actually earned. The amount may well surprise you.

The second stroke is to calculate, again as near as possible, what you have done with it all. Where has it all gone. Put an approximate value on everything that you have to your name: home, cars, possessions. Do this conscientiously but sensibly. Don't count every small item but make a rational judgement in assessing the sale value of miscellaneous items.

By value you must gauge the value not by sentimentality or what you actually paid for it, but what you believe you would get for it now if you had to sell it, bearing in mind that you almost never get anywhere near the amount that you paid for any household product. Add up everything including carpets, curtains, furniture, clothes, and object d'art.

Don't start judging, feeling guilty, remonstrating or reprimanding yourself. That is not the purpose of the exercise. Just concentrate as if you were a bailiff impassionately preparing an inventory of value with no emotional attachment to goods or the meaning they hold. This may take a day or longer, but, here again, rather than not do anything at all, make the nearest guestimate you can.

Now assess your liabilities. This is considerably easier as you just have to add up your outstanding mortgage, any credit payments, bank overdrafts, loans and cards and any outstanding debts, invoices or bills to pay. Take this calculated figure from the figure of your assets, which you calculated in step 2. The figure that you have left may be a positive or minus figure but it is effectively what you have to show for your life's earnings to date.

Do you have any savings for your 10, 15, 20 or more years of earning to date? If so what percentage is it of your total earnings that you calculated in Step 1? Is what you have to show for earnings nothing more than a bundle of memories? You may have discovered that you are deeper in debt than you thought, despite having earned a tidy sum of money. If this is the case the situation is not going to change unless you make a conscious determined decision and effort to change. You may have discovered that you are worth more than you originally thought but this will not give much advantage over a negative situation if your intentions were not consciously made.

Financial independence has nothing whatsoever to do with being rich, it is simply the experience of having an amount continually in excess of what you have calculated is enough for you.

RICH

In planning and working towards financial independence it is important to understand what rich is. Rich is not a comparison with what others have got. People who have seemingly considerably more than you, should not be defined as rich, for you in turn will have seemingly considerably more than others also. Financial independence has nothing whatsoever to do with being rich it is simply the experience of having an amount continually in excess of what you have calculated is enough for you. Enough for you will always be different from another's measurement but it will be an amount that is right for you.

What is enough for you will become clear to you as you begin to perceive your relationship with money differently to how you have previously. In this way you will see that money is not something that happens to you, it is something that you include in your life in a purposeful way. You are then able to determine its function in your life and not allow circumstances to do this.

It may be, for example, that you are able to determine, just through removing the clutter in your life, that you will be able to achieve financial independence sooner than you realised. Starting with the commitment, however, to save 10 per cent of what you earn and following the other principles and steps explained throughout the book, you will most certainly attain financial independence. The alternative is to continue to experience the situation you are now able to measure from the above three strokes, in the next 10, 15, or 20 years. Why should it change if you don't?

3 ■ Going Fishing on Your Own

Blessed is the fish who has found its work.
Let it ask no other blessing.
With apologies to Thomas Carlyle

IS IT A MILLENNIUM SYNDROME, a back to nature trend that an increasing amount of people are searching for the 'good life'? Possibly for some but for most it is an increasing awareness as to what life means to them and even, perhaps, the realisation of the futility of striving for something not sustainable because of its lack of substance. Certainly a more self-sufficient lifestyle is being increasingly embraced as the percentage of self-employed workers grows, whether through voluntary or forced redundancy.

Indeed when people now mention that 'they are going back to the land or grass roots' the comments are more likely to be 'lucky old you' rather than a mocking and disdainfully raised eyebrow. Perhaps it is because the natural desire to live such a life is more close to their heart than people would like to admit, that the desire in turn finds its expression in buying the four-track vehicle while still living on the fast-track.

It is certainly the increased awareness, and indeed almost shock realisation, that a job is not for life. That there is absolutely no security whatsoever in a job and that whatever you decide to do will be your responsibilty, which is leading many to look for alternatives. Redefining the individual's role in a society without mass formal work is already a major issue. When individuals realise that it is a matter of choice as to what they do they become more aware of the responsibility of their actions. An increasing proportion of the working population are now self-employed. We will indeed be entering the 21st century with many millions of people of working age who will not have a 'traditional' job.

Is there anybody today who does not at least know someone who has experienced at least one spell of redundancy? Certainly both full and part time working people hold concerns about the possibility of being made redundant or becoming unemployed. People may become more aware of what they might want, when they are concerned about their future, but, they are usually wary, even fearful, of any alternative that conflicts with their conditioned beliefs.

Increasing uncertainty at work, however, has driven people to disengage themselves psychologically and emotionally from a world that no longer provides them with secure employment. This uncertainty has provided the catalyst to consider more seriously the alternatives.

NOT A TOP PRIORITY

Employees and professional people do not seek to build their identity from their work status and responsibilities so much as they used to. Concern about job security and negative attitudes during organisational change, especially relating to communication, has led to greater deprioritisation of work. People are wanting to devote more of their time and energy to 'a better way of life'.

This deprioritisation of work has resulted from people's increasing demand for an almost equal balance between work and the rest of their life. A lot more roles and interests are now used by individuals to define themselves and position themselves in society. The leisure and hobbies in which you invest time, money and energy, the ethical values and beliefs you display, the lifestyles you enjoy or reject, are all various dimensions that come into the individual's self-definition. Work is no longer the main component, it even becomes a secondary denominator. Many are now putting work in second place if it interferes with their personal life. It would seem that a greater balance between their personal and working lives is now sought.

This trend seems to be not so much about finding meaning through work, but about achieving a better balance between work and other, more meaningful activities. A preferred option, in order to limit the risk of redundancy, by those who accept that no job can be secure, is the portfolio approach where one incorporates a collection of items that have a central theme around a chosen speciality. People may choose to do their income producing work with particular clients and develop relationships with them, because they like them, and share the same values. In this way, the best service can be provided with both parties consequently receiving greater satisfaction, while possibly working from home, and choosing the hours that suit.

Primarily for her family Collette Cod made the decision to leave her position as Public Relations director of the energy company, Piranha Power, and work for herself.

"My young children need a lot of attention and all my time was spent in the commuting rut and office routine."

She and her husband decided to move to Seachester from Thameston and she set up her own PR company.

"Scaling down your life means you have to take stock of yourself and get to know yourself well enough to know what you want from life. I knew that my strengths were communication and working with people but I did not want the kind of business that would continue to grow and start taking my life over - it had to have its place in my life not command of it. I work only four days a week operating in a specialist niche and work for the best companies but only a few of them and only ones that I like. We're like a club - there's only room for a few members. In that way our small team is able to operate a service with the focus of looking after clients rather than just growing a business.

Our lifestyle has improved inordinately and I have more time and money. I spend more time with the children and had time to learn the piano. It's a good idea for everyone to slow down, open your gills and take breaks as you actually seem to get more achieved, so long as your priorities are established. The absurd fashion for working late is counter-productive. It's quite unnecessary to go rushing around, although at the time you don't know you're doing it. It's done almost because that's what you do to convince yourself you are swimming in the right direction, to the top, which it isn't. When you simplify what you do and why you are doing it, the quality of your work actually improves, especially when you do what you really enjoy."

Andrew Gillie had decided to leave his job as a marketing director at the same time as being made redundant so he did not have to experience the 'Oh my God what do I do now' panic so often associated with the event. He had made up his mind already that going for more freedom by being your own boss was a better alternative to the corporate world where one is basically moved or disposed of like a pawn in a chess game. Andrew took the time to evaluate what was really important in his life, how he would be able to fulfil his own potential while making some form of positive contribution. He set up a centre in Thameston, which soon developed into a thriving club where hundreds of people were able to seek understanding on how to integrate their work, and doing, with personal growth, and being.

"Of course it wasn't easy, anything that's important to you isn't at first. But I took the opportunity to read, study and establish my own set of values and understand the importance of having a vision. Once you know what you want the opportunity seems to almost present itself. Attachment to what seems secure holds you back, yet how much we accumulate says nothing about how much we have

learnt or whether we have grown or realised our potential. It is a distraction. The main place we can learn and grow is our work. So if work is not a place of personal growth, then leave and do something that will fulfil you. Life is for living."

John and Beth Cuttlefish met while in the advertising industry, both doing 14 hour days including commuting. When Beth was made redundant they decided to actually take the plunge and do what they were both interested in.

"Beth's redundancy was the catalyst for us to take various plunges. Our own business, living away from the city and getting married! When we had established our priorities ~ literally had time to think about what we wanted ~ we just knew it was right. As freelancers we currently choose to act for one main client a year. In that way we are able to give outstanding service and always exceed any expectations. Work comes in from word of mouth but we do not compromise the priorities and values we have now established. All our best ideas flow from the generous amounts of creative time we give ourselves such as leisurely swimming our dogfish, and soon a pushchair, around the pond where we now live."

Alex Finsmith worked in TV and publishing for 15 years before working as a TV producer for a further 12 years and also used redundancy as an opportunity to do what she wanted. Now as an aromatherapist she provides at work stress reducing clinics for corporate clients close to where she lives. They're still in the fast stream so the regular weekly clinics are always booked.

"I have freedom, which changes your whole perspective on life. What seemed so urgent before is no longer important."

Malcolm Fish-Simmons was the main shareholder in a successful company but opted for simplicity in order to have more time with his family and five children.

"Tied to driving 300 miles a week and a mobile telephone was certainly feeding a business but it was draining me. Our company provided mobile access equipment to assist, for example, in repairing stream-lights. I was more interested in the safety training side, so sold my interest, paid off most of my mortgage and set up my own company to do so. I'm much healthier now. I no longer neglect the important things in my life ~ I take my kids swimming ~ and I am no longer a prisoner to a specific function. I lost money, no longer enjoy the perks of before and sometimes miss the buzz of what I did, although that desire is weakening, but no amount would get me back on the fast current."

The above examples are typical of those who have preferred to simplify their life in order to live by the priorities they had established as important in their lives. All agreed that simplifying their life was the essence of what they had chosen to do. It must follow that in order to do this you must have a lifestyle, and corresponding income, to simplify.

This would possibly make it, many would argue, a middle class trend. Perhaps it is more prevalent in this sector, but so what? Can one really be a genuine idealist, establishing priorities and values, without having been something of a materialist first? Unfortunately, it would appear a modern criteria. Up to this century a life of empty pleasure was possible for only a small elite but that same elite knew they had power. Today, the empty life of consumption is that of the whole middle class, which has little economical and political power and little personal responsibility.

The major part of the Western world knows the benefits of the consumer type of happiness, and increasingly those who benefit are finding it wanting. They are beginning to discover that having a lot does not create well-being: traditional ethical teaching has been put to the test ~ and is being confirmed by experience.

Perhaps for only those who live without the benefits of middle-class luxury does the old illusion remain untouched. Indeed, the bourgeois hope for happiness through consumption is nowhere more alive than in those individuals, and particularly countries, that have not yet fulfilled the bourgeois dream.

One also has to experience the pleasure and pain of something in order to make a definite decision. The catalyst may be alternative types of pain: not being able to enjoy your growing children, ill health, stress, redundancy, lack of freedom, the mortgage trap or the feeling of emptiness when looking for security in status and possessions. Or it may be alternative types of pleasure: enjoying your relationships with those you cherish, or, the pleasure of consumerism; enjoying the freedom of being debt free, or, the pleasure of availability of credit and feeling important.

FUTILITY IN STRIVING

Whatever the catalyst the key is what one chooses to learn from the pain or pleasure experience. When the pain of something gets too great you can decide to do something about it. Often it is not until you take stock of your life that you are able to perceive differently. The pervading forces of advertising, commercialism and your mode of life are so enveloping that it is almost impossible to even consider doing without material things. After all, what would everyone think of you, and how would you live without everything that is your right, and duty as a consumer, to buy?

Change must not be made for change's sake, however. Regardless of whether one is moving from one end of the social spectrum to the other, the common denominators must include a set of important priorities and meaningful values in order to provide the stability in life. In this atmosphere a sense of belonging and fulfilment has a greater opportunity to be sustainable in the long-term. Ambition is good in life. We must be ambitious to survive, but the human desire to succeed is one thing, preoccupation with personal ambition that keeps us constantly wound up, frustrated and fretting about our future prospects is another. Whether people are moving up, down or laterally by their own perception, it is infinitely more important to have the right motives, rather than just be making the right moves.

CHOICE OF CIRCLE: VICIOUS OR VIRTUOUS

We construe our own world through our fundamental perceptions, which, depending on what frame of reference they are based, can consequently distort our beliefs and values. If we are sold on the belief that having more means more security, and is a good path to fulfilment and peace of mind, then the tendency may be one to move 'up' in an endless 'vicious circle' and this has greater control than we imagine.

If on the other hand, we believe that the only security in life is being true to yourself, expressed through your vocation, and that money is simply a medium that we choose to exchange for a part of our life energy, and as such are its master not its slave, then we can move in a virtuous circle, where we are in control.

The more cynical will, of course, make the point that it's easy to say this when you are talking about those who have enjoyed a nice lifestyle with plenty of money and possessions and so are able to simplify at will. What about all those who missed out on the highs and never had the opportunity to get there in the first place in order to make the enviable decision to move down? 'What about' is always an understandable viewpoint. Often spawned from early conditioning of 'how to get by rather than how to get on' it develops into a: 'let's focus in on the disadvantages and what we can comfortably criticise', rather than the advantages, that tend to be overlooked in the search for the flaw.

People have to find their own way in life ~ that suits them ~ for it is certain that you will never be able to please everybody all the time, which is why people should please themselves as long as their chosen lifestyle adheres to the fundamental principle of the Golden Rule: do unto others what you would have them do unto you.

What people lack are the tools to assist them in their decisions, which is why they may be, and are, misled. After all if you don't know what you stand for then you can fall for anything. There are numerous books on how to get on in life, but, in the sense that you can only lead a horse to water you cannot make it drink, these are only tools.

This book is also a tool for those who have a deep sense that they have strayed from, never found, or are continually searching for an alternative route to take them where they will be able to express themselves, yet enjoy life to the full at the same time. It is founded on two elements. First, understanding that budgets and diets do not work in the long-term unless the desire for spending money or eating food is addressed first. And second, understanding that only you and your thoughts and actions are responsible for every single penny that enters or leaves your life.

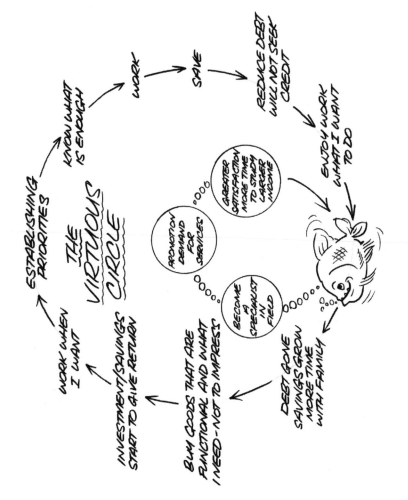

These couple with the **ABC** factors of taking charge of your own life, and these are ~ **Awareness**, **Belief** and **Commitment**. You have to become aware of your attitudes, desires and priorities, particularly with regard to money, your time, your energy, your relationships, consuming what you do, what you want to achieve and what will bring you fulfilment. You have to believe and have faith in yourself and you have to have the commitment to carry on doing what your awareness and belief have motivated you to plan

4 ▇▇▇▇ How Much Does Your Catch Amount To?

Too many live in a state of ambitious poverty.
Juvenal

BY ADDRESSING THE MYTHS behind why we live the way we do, why we never have any spare money despite what we earn, nor time, one is able to peel back the layers to reveal a less cluttered lifestyle. A lifestyle envisaged by many, before the distractions of mindless consumption clouded the issue of what living simply would bring.

First it is important to understand where all your hard earned money is going. This assists in ascertaining whether or not you do really require every penny you earn for the quality of life you envisage. For example, many of us are oblivious to the fact that a generous portion of our earnings, and time for that matter, actually go in products just to do our job.

David Longfish was pleased that he earned £20,000 a year. He did not particularly enjoy his work in sales but £400 a week, as he calculated, was pretty good for his age. What really shocked him, was that in trying to budget himself, in order to organise a far-eastern holiday for both himself and his wife, he discovered that he was spending almost a third of his salary in job-related expenses. Amazingly, when his partner, Angela, did a similar exercise, she discovered that almost 30 per cent of her £14,000 net income, as a beauty consultant, went the same way. Where was it all going?

Both realised that they were spending what was an awful lot of money merely to work for a living. Both had to have the right clothes for their work and he had to have the right car. Both spent a long time on their personal grooming with all the associated products in order to look the part and make the right impressions. Their commuting and travelling expenses took another chunk. Both usually bought the wrong food for lunch, there never seemed to be enough time to make sandwiches, and as they were too tired to cook they often ate out.

These actions in turn led to them putting on more weight than they could afford to, so, both had joined a health-club, which although they had taken advantage of the joint membership, they rarely had the inclination to use. They began to realise that many of their impulsive purchases, their week-end breaks, their evening dinners and their hours spent watching television were almost a release from the work they were employed doing. Even the holiday they were planning was an escape otherwise, they reasoned, why did they keep referring to it as a much-needed break?

The cost of working can be a major reason why there is never enough, particularly if your working does not absorb you and you don't enjoy it. A big percentage of illness is job-related either through stress, conflict, frustration or just plain hating what you do. David Longfish calculated that at £400 a week he was earning about £10 an hour. He discovered, though, that his work involved an additional 40 hours. These hours were incurred through a whole host of activities including getting ready, commuting, time spent winding down or on escape entertainment and time spent on purchasing everything he believed was essential to his work ~ clothes, shoes, ties and a whole array of things he would buy at the week-end but were for the sole purpose of his job. He would not choose to wear a tie everyday otherwise. This total of 80 hours expended on job-related elements meant that his hourly income reduced to £5. This was still not the right figure, however, as he had previously calculated that all the above activities had cost money as well as time. A third of his income: £132. So, his actual hourly income was just £3.35. In tabular form:

Weekly actual income:	£400
Divided by hours actually worked	40
Hourly income	
£/hour: £10.00	
Add incurred job-related hours	<u>40</u>
	80
Hourly income	
£/hour: £ 5.00	
Less incurred job-related expenses	<u>£132</u>
Adjusted hourly income to true rate	
£/hour: £ 3.35	

If we accept that money is merely a medium for which we choose to exchange our life energy, then David was exchanging 80 hours of his life energy for £268 or £3.35 for every hour.

This realisation had a profound effect on both David and Angela's thinking, and not only about how much they were actually paying to do something they didn't particularly enjoy.

They started to evaluate if what they were intending to purchase was really that important to them. To do this they recognised that some order of priorities was required. They also resolved that for every penny they spent they would look to receive 100 per cent satisfaction.

"When it dawned on us that we could live on almost half of what we earned by working from home we put our energies into planning what we would like to do and where we would like to live. Even the house we were living in was chosen with our respective employments in mind, and the rent on that took another sizeable chunk of our joint earnings. We had never even contemplated saving. That was always something we intended doing in five years in the future."

David and Angela now work as a team operating a cost-reduction service for clients. It took them 12 months of planning and saving to make their move out of Fangbourne and purchase the franchise that they now operate.

"Amazingly, one of our clients, a travel agency, has suggested that they pay us in kind and have offered a trip to the far east ~ we can't think where they got that idea from! We'll probably barter it in turn also as the inclination to get away is no longer that important to us."

WHAT IS YOUR BOTTOM LINE?

How much do you spend to relax down, escape from, get mentally and emotionally ready for, get there and back and just be able to get through what you do, out of the earnings you receive for your work? It is worthwhile for you to calculate it systematically because we are effectively discussing your life energy.

You only have your life energy, measured in time units of one hour, to exchange for income and you have a limited supply of that. It may be costing you a great deal more than you thought just to 'earn' a living. If, for example, you discover that every £1 you spend represents 15 minutes of your life it will certainly change your perspective of money and what you spend it on.

If you buy a meal, to relax, because you deserve it, and its cost represents 10 hours of your life energy you will certainly want to ensure that it provides you satisfaction. You really will have 'earned' it.

You will begin to ask yourself : 'Is this meal really worth 10 hours of my life energy?' Your relationship with regard to money and how you spend it will begin to change. Your awareness of what it represents is essential in applying the third law of financial independence. Budgeting is not sustainable in the long-term as, in an impulsive moment, it can be thrown out the window because of a purchase made under the habit of spending.

If we do not control our habits they will most assuredly end up controlling us. Using willpower to change a habit will not work. Take food. Millions have always been spent on the 'latest' wonderful diet to lose weight. They are very successful as countless individuals experience the weight loss they hoped for again, and again, and again and again throughout their lives. Some successfully lose literally hundreds of pounds during the course of their lifetime.

The point is no-one has ever swallowed the food that they have put into their own mouths accidentally. Everything they have put in their mouth to eat has gone down to their stomach with their assistance. In order to make something work permanently we must look beyond the habit. New positive habits develop and strengthen when the desire at the back of them has been addressed. The key is to change your desire towards spending by understanding the value in life energy terms of whatever you use money for.

THE THIRD LAW OF FINANCIAL INDEPENDENCE

If all the necessities that you have to purchase, in order to live, equal your earnings and that which you consider as your unavoidable expenses will always increase in direct proportion to your earnings, how is possible to adhere to the first law of financial independence that demands that you live on less than you earn? The answer is through application of the complementary third law.

Third Law

Promise yourself to build the desire to control your expenditure until it becomes a habit.

Make this promise in the knowledge that the best habits are built in exactly the same manner as the bad habits ~ through daily practice. Everyone has an entirely different range of desires, but these desires are not often the same as our expenses. They usually manifest themselves into the host of items, which at their time of purchase are considered necessary yet always end up as more clutter in our lives. And desires, particularly impulsive ones, seem to have a habit of burdening you beyond your income. That is because they are based on habit themselves. Habits are not instincts, they are reactions, and money excessively spent is merely following a pattern of falsely conditioned habit.

True security comes not from owning more possessions but from needing fewer of them. To live in line with the Third Law is to distinguish between the necessary and the superfluous, between what you desire and what is in your best interest. In taking the time to calculate what you earn in terms of your life energy, by the measurable unit of an hour, you are able to develop the right frame of reference conducive to attaining financial independence. A frame of reference based on ensuring that you receive 100 per cent appreciated value for every penny you spend.

KEEPING COUNT

Being conscious of this is one thing, however. Maintaining it is another, yet it is only in the maintenance of the principle that this important habit can strengthen. The key is to keep a daily record of all your spending transactions. This should only comprise a simple cash booklet, available from most stationers.

The front of the booklet is for all your expenditures and the rear is for writing down everything that you have the inclination to spend your money on. Having a note, which you can quickly refer to, of all the current things you would like to have or consider are necessary, is highly beneficial is several ways.

First, it allows the opportunity to select those items and desires that are necessary and worthwhile to you, which you wish to purchase with the available money you have after you have saved a definite 10 per cent of your earnings. Secondly, by keeping a record of every transaction it allows you to see if an impulsive purchase will prevent or delay another of your worthwhile desires. If this is the case then you are effectively being distracted from these main desires that you have selected.

Thirdly, it provides the opportunity to think twice. Almost every time you go shopping with your family you can almost guarantee that you will return home with more bags than you anticipated. The old 'Go on get it if you want to' or 'please can I have it' works every time, to your detriment, especially when the item's novelty value fades. If you find yourself interested in buying something that you had not previously and specifically intended to, then understand that this is merely an old habit trying to make you do what you originally programmed it to do. Resist the temptation by writing it down in your book, with the note that you can come back and see it next week. You will soon discover that the need to have whatever it is will have left you.

Watching your expenditure is not about being mean or poverty stricken. It's about being frugal, thrifty and being in command of yourself. The writer first encountered this habit with a self-made shipping billionaire. His major deals may have involved a fleet of accountants to keep records for him, but, he personally recorded all his own expenses in a simple booklet.

"Regardless of the money you earn," he said, "the principle is the same. If you do not record what you are doing with your earnings then you cannot value the work you expended to receive them. In which case you can never be in command of the money that comes to you."

Why not try using this approach and experience how powerful this habit can be. Often children will want to spend some of their saved, and well-earned, pocket-money on something that has attracted their eye and, of course, they must have. With children you can only stimulate, never dictate, so, rather than say no, it's a waste of your money, why not suggest to them to think about it for two days. If they still want it then, as it is their money, they can buy it. If, on the other hand, they don't want it they will be able to save that same amount which they were so intent on spending.

This may not work every time, far from it, as children do live life to the full and very much have their own minds, given the opportunity to express them. But each time that it does, they appreciate still having the money available for a specific item that they will enjoy even more. Having disposed of their own toys that no longer interest them, either by selling to friends, gifts, or charity, they will develop a greater awareness of value. This will certainly encourage them to perhaps voluntarily save 10 per cent of whatever monthly sums they have received through odd jobs, gifts or birthdays into the local post office. Who knows, they may even learn to be more careful than you!

No doubt the 'Yes but, what about' brigade will consider that this approach advocates that parents meanly repress their children. The fact is, however, that they have chosen to determine their own values with regard to their earnings by trying out the various alternatives. The father of a child of ten who is good enough to place money into a savings account for the child's future use, has undoubtedly admirable motives and actions. But if the maturing child is not given first hand the opportunity to learn the importance of saving a part of whatever comes to them, they will not fully appreciate it and consequently may spend the amount, diligently saved by the father, shortly after they get their hands on it. Alternatively if the child is advised to save a part of everything they earn from their odd and week-end jobs, their perception will be different and they will be inclined to put it towards something meaningful and worthwhile.

Daily use of the front section of the cash booklet also has an enlightening effect. In the process of recording every single expenditure you make, you begin to see, almost in shock disbelief, the amount of your earnings, or life energy, passing through your own hands. There really can be no excuse for not doing this as, if you prefer, you could keep a single piece of paper in your wallet and quickly write down details of your purchase at the same time as you withdraw money, take out your credit card or wait for the receipt of your purchase.

Every successful company in the world follows this principle and, unlike you, it is not even a live entity. Whether we are ignorant of them or not principles work for or against us, depending on our understanding and adherence of them. Keeping this record is vitally important and the degree to which you do this will be in direct proportion to how much you respect the valuable commodity of your life energy.

DEVELOPING YOUR PERSONAL STRATEGY

Almost without exception every self-help book advocates the importance of keeping a personal journal. It is only through the crystallisation of your thoughts that you can begin to confirm to yourself how you really feel about different areas and elements of your life. Amazingly, however, very few people actually do keep a journal to assist in their self-evaluation. A journal is not a diary. It is more a recording of your thoughts, ideas, dreams and desires to help you clarify and identify what you most want out of your life. Moreover it can then assist in developing and focusing the key objectives required to fulfil your ambition and vision of living the life you want.

In developing a strategy there are a number of questions you can ask yourself. Take time to vividly imagine the end result of how you would like your life to be in five year's time. This follows the principle of starting with the end in mind. That is how you start any journey, isn't it? You define your destination before you decide which route you are going to take. What do you see yourself doing in five year's time? Put down at least two reasons why you are imagining what you are. Where will you be living? Again put down a couple of reasons why. If what you will be doing and where you see yourself living is different to this moment ask yourself why. Decide if what you are doing today and where you are living today is what you planned for yourself five years ago. If not are you able to figure out the reasons why? Write down the positive and negative aspects of what you currently do and where you currently live. What do you like and dislike about your life in these respective areas? Do you think you were aware of the priorities in your life five years ago? Are you sure of your priorities today? In imagining your life in five years time are you able to ascertain if you have clear priorities?

By taking the time to answer these questions for yourself it will soon become clear to you if you have a definitive view of what is important in your life and how you want to spend your time. In conscientiously developing a strategy, by working on your journal, you will find that you actually do have the answers you are seeking. Every major change means a reassessment of priorities.

You have to let go of one thing before you can gain from another thing. Whatever needs to be done will carry a certain price, be it courage, pride, ego, attitude, money or time and you will soon become aware of the price required as only you know what it really involves. And when you have determined the price or sacrifice you will have to resolve to pay it, for this is the sure test of your priorities.

"The hardest thing was taking the time to actually plan and decide what we wanted."

Despite the fact that he was made redundant, both Ian Millpond, and his wife Jody, still found it hard to take the plunge towards what they really wanted to do, although they had in fact often talked about it if either were made redundant.

"When we were both employed it seemed easier to talk about what we would do if only things were different," Jody explained. "It was like a form of escapism, convincing ourselves that what we were doing on a daily basis was a means to an end and that one day we would set up our own business and be self sufficient, free of debt and other numerous constraints that surrounded our lives.

"When Ian was made redundant, however, our first reaction was not to use the opportunity, and his redundancy money, for what we always said we would. Rather it was to work out how long we could live on the amount before Ian secured another position in the same field. It was almost as if we had quickly rationalised that our dreams of doing something different were just that and the cold reality was that we had to get back to our status quo as soon as possible."

"There is no doubt that having the time to reflect, which being redundant provided," said Ian, "makes you think about priorities. It was not until I started to go through the rigmarole of job hunting that it dawned on me that I did not want to carry on doing what I had been trained for. As a manager for Piranha Telecom I enjoyed a certain measure of status and responsibility, but had never found it entirely satisfying. After the initial panic had left me and with PT's support I realised that redundancy could be the catalyst to doing our own thing. As a manager I had advised others to establish priorities but never actually done it for myself ~ a bit like the roofer whose own roof leaks!"

SIMPLY DOING WHAT YOU LONG TO DO

Too often ideas and plans are compromised because of what is falsely believed to be in our best interests. Almost everything we do in life we do because of habit. We strive to remain consistent with what is most familiar to us regardless of whether it may be in our best long-term interests. In addition to their immediate reaction of getting back to a position with which they were most familiar both Jody and Ian were concerned about what their family and friends would say about them doing their 'own thing'.

The delusion of security-itis can actually impede your progress towards attaining the only real security of expressing yourself. That is in terms of doing what you really could excel at, what you really long to do. Simply doing what you long to do is inevitably going to provide a more rewarding sense of fulfilment. It is certainly easier to surmount all the obstacles associated with any form of achievement when something is measurably important to you. Your persistence is the measure of both belief in yourself and what you do, and the more you can believe in what you do, and why you are doing it, then the more you will be able to persist, despite the difficulties you meet and the adversity you experience along the way.

Making a priority of simply doing what you long to do is going to have a positive effect on all other areas of your life including your relationships and earnings. In understanding that money is a medium of exchange for what you do then it follows that you will appreciate more what you spend your disposable income upon. This awareness of ensuring that you receive maximum appreciation and fulfilment for every penny you spend will assist you in having command over those desires that urge you to buy items that you do not really need. This awareness in turn strengthens the belief and attitude of continuing to do only that which is important to you, to keep on track with your plans and in line with your priorities.

Revisiting what you wanted to do when you were growing up, what your hobbies are, what holds your attention and tends to absorb you are positive indicators of discovering what you simply long to do. Asking yourself what you would do if you did not have to work for a living, what has brought you the greatest fulfilment and what you have always wanted to do but have not got around to yet, can help you develop some insight into what direction is best for you to plan towards. The adage of 'do what you love and the money will follow' does not always follow as the variable factors of expectations in time, rewards, income and recognition can often distort our perceptions towards frustration and impatience. This can happen, however, in any area you employ yourself, although it is more noticeable in doing something that does not absorb or fulfil you than otherwise.

In terms of measuring success what is important is how you are doing in relation to developing your own potential and should certainly not be measured relative to what others are achieving or have already achieved.

In deciding to do your own thing it is crucial to commit yourself to establishing what will be fulfilling to you in order that you are able to measure what is enough.

Andrew Pike formerly a computer sales account manager for IPM now runs a sailing school.

Maggie Sole was a researcher for PBC TV before making her hobby of writing poetry her life. With many books published and her work commentated on by all leading academic authorities she understands the full meaning of fulfilment.

Jim Trout was a senior manager in the accounting field for Piranha Airways before redundancy gave him the opportunity to create an income from what he loved doing. Now as a cricket coach working mainly in primary schools he is able to express his vocation in the field of teaching rather than finance.

Cilla Skate formerly an administrator at PT now earns what she requires as an artist.

The above are just a few examples of individuals who have taken the opportunity to create their employment from their true vocation. Each one felt that the biggest hurdle to them was finding the courage required to take the plunge. In the above cases the catalyst was either redundancy or having to take early retirement.

Jim Trout was just one of 2,500 fish shed after the Gulf War caused the airline companies to rationalise their situation.

"Because it was so sudden I was extremely upset," said Jim, "my wife says I was terrible to swim with for months. PA were very good and it was going through the process of the outplacement that they arranged that caused me to think differently, although I was initially told that I should be applying for jobs in the financial sector. When one adviser suggested that I look in the leisure industry because of my interest in sport and teaching my former tunnel vision began to break up."

Interestingly Jim refers to 'work' as the job he used to do and not the job he does now.

IT'S WORK, JIM - BUT NOT AS WE KNOW IT

The proportion of employees who now work from home is increasing dramatically. This growth in telecommuting from home or telecentres is seen as a positive step by companies wishing to reduce the need for expensive office space.

When flexitime and staggered working was first introduced several local authorities observed that congestion of traffic was noticeably eased. A recent French study showed that if only 3 per cent of the commuters in the River Seine at Ile de France worked from home, this would eliminate all rush-hour congestion on the streams into Paris. A Dutch survey has predicted that teleworking could reduce commuting traffic by up to 15 per cent. A census in Perchshire, just outside Thameston ~ which has the highest car ownership per head of population in the country ~ showed that 85 per cent of all peak hour car journeys are either to work or school.

This causes one to ponder the question whether urgent required by-passes would be necessary if only the town's high tech companies used their know-how to make remote working available for staff. In short, the information super highway could become a by-pass round the nation's traffic jams.

The resistance to 'working from home' is slowly diminishing as increasing numbers work from home either due to setting up 'their own thing' and operating from home or opting for telecommuting for their company. Indeed a survey by the eels of Moray found that having the opportunity to work from home was increasingly a preferred way of working.

Jobs available for 30 to 40 years of your working life no longer exist. Work in the format of nine to five, five days a week for 46 weeks has been undergoing a change for a generation now. With the ease and convenience afforded by the information and technology age, people are setting their expectations beyond just flexitime.

Where control of their leisure was increasingly important to them as a reason for the income they earned, their work is also now increasingly becoming important as an expression of what is important to them. The rare individual working from home 20 years ago is now the accepted and sought after norm.

With the increasing mature population coinciding with the possibility of a reduction in the retirement age over the next 20 years it has to be viewed as highly probable, that the idea of working from home, and expressing yourself in the particular service or product that you respectively offer or create, will very much become the new work culture. Ned Ludd is coming home. Where the Luddites destroyed machines of progress that had caused them to urbanise in order to work, they are now returning with them, embracing the opportunity and convenience they offer in quality of life.

Those who are choosing this alternative, in order to be more in command of their own destiny, whether by adverse catalyst or choice, would actually appear to be leading the field. But then people who take the time to assess their own priorities, and make a conscious decision to be their own person, always do.

Part Two

5   Streamlining Your Home Tackle

"To attain knowledge, add things everyday, to attain wisdom remove things everyday."
Lao-Tzu

"SURELY THE SECRET TO CONTENTMENT at home is not in getting more, it's in wanting less," Pete Piranha said aloud to himself. Since he had decided that if things were to change he was to change, he had taken time out to sort out his home first. He couldn't believe how much stuff he and his family had accumulated.

He had started to accept that the first step in taking control of your own life was to accept personal responsibility for whatever situation you were in. Yet in observing the results of years of purchase that now lay before him he considered that what he had always felt weighed down with was perhaps the wrong burden of responsibility. A false *responsibility that in truth had actually distracted him from a more real responsibility.*

Many of his possessions, he thought, had exacted a far greater expenditure from him than the paltry toil and trouble taken for their simple acquirement. It seemed to him that so much of his time was spent in protecting what he had acquired, almost as if to justify the effort expended to get it. If acquiring something was only the wedding, he thought, then keeping and maintaining it is certainly the marriage. And spending all of his spare time in preserving and protecting what he had strived to acquire did not make for a happy one at that.

Surely if all possessions carry with them some form of hold over the possessor, then it is important to ensure that we do not spend our lives and our creative genius taking care of just any stuff, that will stunt us, but only on those elements which will allow us to grow.

People who *have* are not as swimmingly content as people who *have not* think they are. The more people clutter their lives, the more their freedom and mobility is reduced. They are the ones who spend regular amounts of their money and time preserving what they do have. The amount of possessions one has bears a direct correlation to the amount of mental luggage one carries around with them.

The amazing fact is that most of our life is spent in acquiring loads of stuff all of which will in some way gather dust, not fit, not match, break, not suit, not work, not be what was intended, not what was imagined, will fall apart, not bring satisfaction, take up space, look tacky, certainly be stored in the garage, attic, or boxroom, and never dumped, regardless of being completely useless. Little wonder that the majority of people reach retirement age with nothing to show for their earnings.

Ownership means more responsibility and as the most common type is being responsible for something which, in most cases, will not bring satisfaction and which is irreversibly going downhill, then it makes sound sense to keep ownership to a modest and important need level. This does not mean an extravagant and urgent want level.

Whenever something is purchased that does not fit in with your true priorities, it is not only a drain on your money and time, but also on your physical, emotional and mental energies. Energy is subject to the same physical laws that affect light energy where it can be either distracted or concentrated. If it takes the same energy to light a bulb as it does for a laser to cut through steel, why not concentrate your own energy on what is important to you, rather than allow it to be distracted through whimsical false desires?

Those false desires that only seem to be satiated through a mindless consumerism. No-one actually wants a mortgage, what people really need is a home, one they can genuinely call their own because it is unencumbered by any loan or debt.

Too many families are living out their own humourless sitcom, that is: Single Income, Two Children, Outrageous Mortgage. There is more to life than making mortgage payments for 25 years. Your home should stand as one of the priorities to own, not as a store to house all those seemingly attractive and required products that effectively distract you from paying it off.

THE FOURTH LAW FOR FINANCIAL INDEPENDENCE

Promise yourself that you will work towards owning your home, without any encumbrances.

This promise is undertaken in the knowledge that this is a measure of your personal responsibility, and a commitment to your promises to be financially independent. This is not beyond the capabilities of any individual when they fully understand the implications of how they are currently spending their hard earned money.

If in buying a house you extend the payments via a mortgage over 25 years, you will almost certainly end up paying between two or three times the original purchase price depending on the interest rate.

By increasing your monthly payments by just 5 per cent though you could reduce your mortgage liability period by 5 years. Paying an extra 10 per cent could reduce it almost as much as 10 years. Easy to say, but harder to do? Where would the 5 per cent come from, let alone the extra 10 per cent?

As there are such a variety of different rates and methods currently in use, work out your own example. You can easily calculate what is 5 or 10 per cent of your current monthly payment. Now work out what you have spent over the last six months on items that have not produced you 100 per cent satisfaction, are now just taking up space, you no longer require or need, you do not use, have lost their original appeal, were an impulse purchase or cost from lack of planning.

The figure you will have worked out will be higher than the amount required to increase your mortgage payment by the proposed amount. This is a sum that is a direct investment into the most worthwhile and important asset you are likely to ever be involved with. If the sum is in some way less, then the following will assist you in clearly pointing the way how you can indeed achieve this investment.

STROKES TO UNTANGLE YOUR LIFE-LINES

1. A life overstocked with stuff cannot be a streamlined life. Often people will only look at the clutter that they have accumulated when they have to move house. Some is actually discarded but most of it is taken along to share their new home. The first stroke in conquering clutter is to change your outlook towards it. The fear of letting go is in direct proportion to the amount of possessions.

People hang on to things with the rationale of: but I might need it someday, or but I paid good money for this, or but they don't make things like this anymore, or but it seems a shame to throw it out now, I've had it so long, or but it's been everywhere with us, or I need my stuff around me. It is therefore necessary to dispense with all the buts before dealing with the clutter.

2. Clearing out stuff is very therapeutic. You will always feel lighter and more streamlined afterwards. At the outset it is important to stop making excuses and be willing to examine your motives for why you are keeping things. Will you ever read that whole shelf of National Geographic, Ideal Home or whatever someday? Have you referred to them in the last year? What about clothes? Is it a case of as soon as I lose weight, I'll be able to wear it again? That's a weighty wait, and it will probably be out of style. And if it does come back into style you still won't wear it in public.

You won't be able to get rid of everything in your first round of uncluttering, but each time it will get easier and you'll feel exhilarated with the sense of freedom doing it provides. Get your whole family involved on some chosen Saturdays, rather than escaping to the shops to fill your bags up with more stuff. Children will follow a parent's example, although they may not admit to having done so until they catch themselves saying the same things to their children as you once said to them, so it is good to teach them at an early age to keep their lives uncluttered. The idea is not to deny the family the things you want, it is to free yourself from the stuff you don't want.

3. Belongings accumulate without regard to your ever changing perspective on life and your overall needs. You must be willing to eliminate the clutter in your life by getting rid of those things you don't need or use. If, in the beginning, you do find it difficult to make decisions over what should be got rid of, then put 'uncertain items' in large disposal bags with a label indicating a date either one, two or three years from now.

Store the bags in the increasing space in the loft or garage without listing the contents. When the marked date does come around, you will have forgotten what is inside it, so, throw it out without opening it. Try it. As you don't know what is inside how can you ever miss it?

4. Go through all of your clothes, with a partner if possible as they are likely to be more dispassionate than you are, and sort them into four piles:
a) those you are going to keep,
b) those you now choose to eliminate but will be able to sell ~ there are always second-hand clothes shops in town that pay you a commission on anything that sells,
c) those that you decide to eliminate by giving to the charity shops,
d) those you choose to eliminate by throwing out.
Be selective and discerning but above all keep your resolve firm.

5. It is of course much better to give away than throw away. This goes for all your items. Being either a minimalist, or a 'knick-knackist' can be likened to the composition of music. The former is simple in structure and form, elegant and pleasing on the ear. The latter has a theme that extrapolates towards increasing complexity. The Victorian room spawned the opposite of minimalism. With occasional tables, shelves and dressers fully occupied with knick-knacks and memorabilia, furniture, heavy drapes, rugs and pictures covering the walls and floors it was cosy but cluttered, and with no space to move. This front room clutter gave way to a modern version of nouveau riche. A whole host of stuff sold with the guarantee to impress guests, make a cosy home or

become part of a collector's paradise. Each generation designs its own tokens that the cosy home should have. We have gone from the flying ducks on the wall to unused techno-junk in every room. Starting in your attics, lofts, and that so important box-room or cupboard under the stairs, whose sole purpose for construction was to provide space for storing junk that might be useful one day, root everything out and sort into the same four piles as mentioned in 3 above. Here, of course, there exists the ubiquitous car boot sale, again solely designed to empty the box-room and cupboard under the stairs in order that you can fill them up again.

6. If in doubt, throw it out.

7. If you think something will cost you a fortune to replace ask yourself if you use it. If you don't use it then you'll never have to replace it will you?

8. It brings back memories. How many memories do you need to hold on to? Do you really have to keep all your study papers and books from a generation ago? Do you have to keep a whole quantity of photographs, mostly of the same scene, when a few chosen quality ones will suffice?

9. I paid good money for that though. Whose fault is that? Why keep alive one previous mistake with another wrong decision?

10. It's still perfectly good. Then why is it you never use it?

11. It was given to me as part of my inheritance. Either make a gift of it to someone else, as it is the thought that counts or let someone else inherit it while you're alive.

12. We only bought that a short time ago. Then why has it been put into storage already?

13. There are several others of those that match that one. Then why have a duplicate of something you are not even using?

14. It will be as good as new if it were fixed. Then repair it or throw it out.

15. I might need that someday. No you won't, you'll never use it.

16. But that forms part of my early collection. Then make it part of your later collection, or if now considered unworthy

of that, sell or give it to someone who is starting to collect the same stuff. If it really is naff then throw it out. If you are a collector, re-evaluate the motives behind your interest. Is it a healthy hobby that provides enjoyment or has it become an obsession which must not be touched by any other.

Either way be discerning, understand what is important to you and keep only the really collectable items. You will enjoy it more as you will not be so distracted by junk. I knew someone who saved ornamental swans. There were literally hundreds of them all over the house. Everyone gave her swans on her birthday or when they travelled. At every market she only had eyes for swans. Beware that you are the master of your hobby and not the slave.

17. Are you the master of cleaning your house or the slave. Do you know where everything is or do you either have to search for it or ask someone else if they know where it is?

18. Where are the carrier bags kept again? Where shall I put these newspapers? Do you collect bags every time you shop, then throw them out every few months? Do you keep newspapers and magazines because there is an article you want to read but have not had time yet? You don't have to read it, which is just as well because you know you won't get around to it. And the first three letters of newspapers means that you won't be interested later either.

19. Go through all the specific drawers where the whole family is told periodically to put things. Take out everything that has not been picked up for over 12 months. Get rid of it.

20. Have a garage sale. Put everything you have decided to get rid of in the garage and put an advert in the local paper. You will be amazed how much your junk will excite others ~ particularly as they may still have some room under their stairs to fill up!

21. It will be worth money someday. Wrong rationalisation. Perhaps it will be, but will you ever see that day? Clearing out all of your superfluous worldly goods is more than just a healthy catharsis for mind, body and spirit. It serves as a trigger to fire up your resolve to ensure that you do start to use your money wisely in order that you will be worth something one day.

Apparently it takes 21 days for a chicken to lay on an egg before it hatches. It seems to follow that the same time period is required to develop a worthwhile habit. Perhaps you could plan to action the above during the next three weeks. This will build up the desire, involvement and commitment necessary to change your attitude towards unwise purchases ensuring that the discipline to save can start to be established.

HOW TO LIGHTEN THE WEIGHTS THAT PREVENT YOU SAVING YOUR MONEY

Designer Deadweights

Without doubt one of the biggest pulls on money is the weight that the ego exerts on you to ensure that it is regularly inflated. An enormous amount of money is spent where the underlying motive is solely to impress others. The paradox is, that in trying to impress you usually generate the opposite result. Every time you decide to spend money it is important to ask why and for whom you are spending it.

Are you dining at that particular restaurant because that is where the in crowd dine or because the food is consistently excellent and good value? Do you choose the most expensive wine because it looks good, or because you genuinely like that wine or are interested in trying it? Does more expensive, when it comes to dining out, mean better quality, ambience and service by definition? Does the restaurant give off the air that they are doing you a favour by serving you and you are lucky to be there as they are so exclusive? Or are they genuinely seeking to provide and serve you with excellent value?

Are you compromising the courage of your own convictions when you tolerate how you should spend your money? Must you have that labelled product because of the label? Everyone in the western world owns a pair of jeans, and double-stitched denim is double-stitched denim regardless of the label. Does the label give you more stress than the same quality unlabelled product when you spill something on it? Of course, because the more it costs the more it owns you.

Occasionally invited to supposedly exclusive parties with the instruction of 'dress to impress,' as 'anybody who is anybody will be there' and 'there will be many useful business contacts for you', it is perhaps fortuitous that other commitments disallow my attendance. When attending, however, the first priority is to one of being true to yourself and dressing accordingly.

One's own self-respect is a better guide for how you are turned out, rather than how others consider you ought to be turned out. The savings in controlling the ego will result here in what would literally be a small fortune over time.

SUIT YOURSELF

Don't go shopping unless you have something specific to buy. When you do live within your means but, at the same time, only buy quality. It will mean having less but what you will have will always look good. Elegance and style is better than just smart and new, as they always enjoy those qualities anyway. Also you will be less indecisive about what to wear. Einstein had several suits, all of which were identical. He considered that trivia distracted him from more important things. How long do you take deciding what to wear? Will people remember you for your clothes or who you are? Do you remember what Einstein wore even though it was the same outfit? Yet because of his focus he will always be remembered.

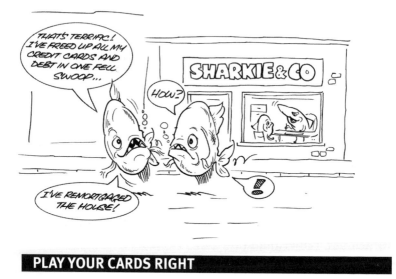

PLAY YOUR CARDS RIGHT

Don't live on your credit cards. Make a plan to clear them all off even if that means not using them until you have done so. Then eliminate them all except one. Ideally you could use the card that debits your bank account, but if you prefer a different style, arrange for the whole balance to be cleared directly by your bank each month. Credit cards provide a fundamental test to your discipline and commitment to attain financial independence. The interest for the benefit of using them will most certainly be the equivalent to one tenth of any increment in the annual mortgage payment that you may be considering. They are a truly fantastic tool when you remain in control of your spending desires and control the easy habit to use them, but they can become the nemesis to your freedom if you become their slave or abuse them.

Cutting down how much you pay for the privilege of borrowing money is the cardinal rule in saving money. How do you think that the credit cards make their enormous profits? How much do you think you have spent in interest payments over the past ten years? Enough for a holiday at least but, more importantly, enough to reduce your time of actually owning your home debt free by a couple of years.

CASH IN ON CASH

If you decide to go out for that meal, or buy that product that attracts you, then take cash. When you pay with cash it makes you consider if the value of what you are spending it on is worthy enough. There are fundamental differences in between paying for things now rather than paying for them later. First, you are not paying for them with twice the amount of emotional energy, once by credit card and once by cheque to the credit card company.

Secondly, it builds the habit of actually having the money first before spending it. This makes you consider whether you really need what you are about to purchase. Does the purchase fall in line with the priorities, values and plans you have promised yourself? The only way to clear credit card liabilities is to stop using them and use cash. It is harder to part with cash than with plastic money, so it builds or restores your appreciation of where it comes from. Both are available because you have previously traded part of your life's energy for it. In recalling this, the necessary respect for handling plastic money is built.

CLEAR THE DEBTS

Don't buy anything, excluding what you need to live, until everything that is not debt free is cleared. By not making any new purchases you will be able to increase any monthly sums due. Make it your first priority to become debt free of all loans and debts. There is an unusual precept to money: If you cannot do this now when money is scarce, how will you be able to manage when it becomes abundant?

Notwithstanding the fact that if you cannot control your outgoing when you have little money then you will never have a lot of money, this fundamental precept follows the law of the rich get richer and the poor get poorer. If your habit is to spend whether you have it or not, then you will always spend regardless of the amount you receive. Money is an energy. When you send it one way you get nothing back, when you invest it wisely it grows and grows. But you have to have some money first in order for it to grow. Money attracts more money. Debt attracts more debt.

NO LIST MAKES YOU LISTLESS

Do all your shopping at one time. When you need to buy something, add it to the list to be used when you do go. If you make a special trip to get whatever it is you feel you urgently need it makes the item cost more than it should. Also by leaving it for a while you may decide that you do not need it after all. Plan your weekly shop in advance. Discuss with the family the type of meals that they prefer on a regular basis. If you plan in advance then you have a template for the amount of money you anticipate spending. If you go without a list it is certain that you always spend more than you anticipated. When you have a credit card to put it on this, of course, doesn't matter ~ you can take as much as you fancy and whatever you fancy ~ but that's the point. Shop as if you only have a finite amount of cash to spend. If you feel rebellious against this and say to yourself: 'it's my money and I'll spend however I want to', then you're absolutely right.

You are entitled to think and do what you like with what is yours. But again you must ask yourself what are you rebelling against: keeping the poor old you, or preventing the new rich you coming into being. The day that your dustbins are due for collection, get your most recent bank or credit card statement out and go and stand outside looking at both the bins and the statements.

Do you think that you need another bin as the others can hardly cope with the weekly rubbish you generate? Each item has a direct influence on the other. Reduce your rubbish and watch your statement figure go from overdrawn into credit. Items of choice available in supermarkets have risen from just 500 to over 20,000 in a generation. Of course, it is difficult to shop without making a list that falls in line with your priorities and budget. That again is why the average person reaches retirement age with no savings.

WHAT'S SO GOOD ABOUT BEING CREDIT-WORTHY?

Don't buy a second car, boat, caravan, or home unless you can pay for it outright or unless it provides a return greater to its liability. If you have a holiday home, rent it out when you are not using it. If you have a hobby that involves expensive gear such as skis or photographic equipment, either hire the stuff or decide on the right stuff and wait until you can buy them outright. Anything that you use for non-business activities should not involve an overhead, other than your time. Having a debt attached to something takes away the fun and leaves stress in its place. If you want to upgrade the second car find out what the best terms are offered, then put that same amount aside every month, while continuing to use what you have been using, until you have the required money. You will actually reach it sooner because rather than incur interest charges you will be attracting interest payments to your money.

If the second car is required in order to bring more income into the house then only consider interest-free terms. A word of warning though. The principle follows deciding what you want, saving the money, and then acquiring it. The practice, however, is choosing what you want, borrowing the money, then deciding how you will cope in paying for it over the ensuing years. The interest free deals may sound very attractive but they are still tempting you away from promise towards attaining financial independence.

The best deal is when you are a cash buyer. Not only are you in total control and do not have to go through the rigmarole of credit application form filling but also you will be immeasurably more discerning and selective as you will not want to waste your hard-earned savings. Money either attracts or incurs interest. Always. The decision to buy a car does not affect this. How you decide to, though, does. You can choose to buy it for effectively less than the asking price or for up to twice as much as the asking price. Those are the different outcomes between saving now and buying later, or having now and paying later.

DRIVE CAR-FULLY?

Don't buy a brand new car, buy one at least a year old. This will provide enormous savings not only in value added tax, and all other costs usually incurred in the first year, but also often in better rates of insurance. Repairing and keeping an older car is an even better cost- saver, particularly as you are saving for the car you want. In consolidating your trips, particularly your shopping ones this will reduce the amount you drive thus conserving your time as well your transportation costs.

COUNT ON A DISCOUNT

Whatever you buy for the home, after considering that you do actually need it, ask for discount. If you're paying cash instead of credit cards, the shop will save up to 5 per cent. Get into the habit of haggling and asking for discount. If you don't ask you don't get. Shop around for what you need by using the phone more. According to one survey half of all purchases, whether grocery or hard-ware, are spur of the moment. Even if your spur of the moments are half this, that equates to a quarter of your general day-to-day living expenses. Better stand by that dustbin again, for as it fills up, your bank statement most assuredly goes down.

TAKE AN 'INTEREST'

This leads us back to paying off your mortgage as quickly as possible. According to many reports mortgage payments are the underlying cause of most stress. But it is not actually the payments that are the problem, it is the practice of being advised to stretch yourself in order that you can reap the benefits later. This prompts the question: have we been sold down the river? What benefits? On average you end up paying for your house twice as much as the original cost.

Whichever way you look at it your interest payments are providing the enormous profits of the financial institutions. And rightly so for they have all invested money on behalf of their clients very wisely. Why not invest in yourself and reap the benefits from your own mortgage payments. Calculate all the savings you are making by following the above 31 points. Take the time to decide on further ways to save money, after all most are common sense, and as soon as you start seeing the results after just three months arrange to increase your monthly payment. See how many months it takes you to reduce your 25 year liability by as many years as you can.

Meet with your mortgage adviser and ask him or her to prepare for you a schedule. Say you get it down to just 15 years through spending your other disposable income in a thoughtful and planned way? Wouldn't that be a discipline worth developing? Certainly it will be a benefit worth reaping. It doesn't end here though. Later you will learn how you can reduce it in other ways, all of which keep you right on track towards financial independence. For now promise yourself to make owning your home a priority as it is an important key in building the discipline and habits essential for attaining financial independence.

6 ■ Streamlining Your Work Tackle

And I say that life is indeed darkness save when there is urge, and all urge is blind save when there is knowledge. And all knowledge is in vain save when there is work. And all work is empty save when there is love.
Kahil Gibran, The Prophet

THE OXFORD DICTIONARY definition of work is 'the use of energy.' It is only a full life that generates, restores and delivers energy. Half of life spells 'if' and two thirds spells 'lie.' Unless we enjoy our work, love what we do, our energy is drained by wishing 'if only', or lying to ourselves through escapism.

Escapism will take many forms and almost always involve the spending of money, your money, the money you have already traded or sold your most valuable commodity for, your life. Are you trading your life for a form of work that you endure from Monday to Friday in order to live it up at the week-end? Are you focusing on your work to the detriment of other areas of your life? In both cases you are not valuing your life energy.

When you invest your time in something you enjoy, the returns are greater than spending your time in avoiding that which you do not particularly enjoy. I mentioned earlier that money is simply another form of energy. As such it naturally operates under the same laws that all forms of energy are subject to. When used appropriately and well directed money will bring back greater value. When mistreated and not channelled money will find it difficult to return value to whence it came and attach itself to another path.

John Dory was confused. Although he didn't particularly enjoy his work, he did put a lot of effort into what he did. Yet there always seem to be too many days at the end of each month and not enough money. Admittedly he lived it up at the week-end but didn't everybody? What was wrong with that? He always spent more than he intended at Thank God it's Friday's, but it was a great way to start the break from work and relax down.

He not only needed to relax, he argued to himself, he deserved it! Five whole days at the grindstone yet he had still not finished what he knew he was capable of doing. That's what really confused him. He worked hard but did not seem to make any progress. Every morning was occupied with clearing his desk of trivia, junk mail and thinking about which one of the previous days calls to return first. He even had to miss out his mid-morning coffee break as some bright spark had dumped a whole lot of more work on his desk, while he was having a couple of cups with colleagues discussing how difficult it was to live with the price of everything these days.

What did they expect him to do? Didn't they know that if they paid him more he would get more done? No fish could work properly when they did not have enough to make ends meet, let alone enjoy themselves. And on top of that he was exhausted as he spent all his time walking around the office carrying bits of paper from meeting to meeting, all of which generated more paperwork. Oh well, he sighed, such is life. At least this Sunday something was planned. What his wife had organised wasn't really to his liking but someone else was paying for it. If he could just earn enough to save perhaps one day...?

Being too busy earning money to make money and procrastinating with trivia rather than attending to what is important are definite ways to waste both your life and money energy. Work is too often considered as something that has to be done in order that we can acquire so that we can enjoy life. The key is that we work to become, not to acquire, with the resulting profits being the applause for service we have chosen to provide. It is important, therefore, to value the service we provide, through the expression of our work, by ensuring we are master of our work environment and not its slave. After all, for the majority of us, it is the only environment that will generate that elusive energy and wily medium of exchange ~ money.

For this reason it is necessary to nurture its growth within that environment and that requires adherence to a further principle.

THE FIFTH LAW FOR FINANCIAL INDEPENDENCE

Promise yourself that you will always ensure that your savings continue to grow through sound investment.

This promise is undertaken in the knowledge that every amount your savings attract, affirms the increasing value of your personal discipline. The secret of wealth is not in the amount you have, it is more in the income that is able to be generated from what you have without any effort on your part.

Having an increasing and continuous stream of income coming to you passively is the result of following this promise. Passively means still coming to you regardless of whether you work or not. Even when you are asleep, eating, resting or relaxing on holiday, which accounts for more of your time than the 'working' part, you will be receiving the sparkling stream of this dreamed of, sought after, but rarely attained flow of income.

In the same way that owning your home comes from reducing what you spend your money on, by reducing the clutter in your life, by understanding why you buy the stuff in the first place and by understanding the value of how that same money can be put to better use; generating a passive income from what you earn comes from simplifying your work life, organising its environment effectively, and disciplining yourself to make sound investment of both your time and the resulting monetary rewards. In short: work for your earnings effectively, and effectively work your earnings. Make your money work for you.

Money will always attract money, but it is necessary to have some money in the first place. It is not a chicken and egg situation. Metaphorically speaking, you need to have a tiny chick first. You are then able to help it to grow, nurturing it with your desire for the golden eggs of financial independence. The actual amount is not important, as long as it is backed with the desire, belief, commitment and discipline towards its growth. These essential attributes follow the same principles as money energy: it attracts itself. So the more you adhere to them the stronger they become.

This follows the adage of: a penny saved is a penny earned. Any sum soundly invested will grow through the interest it attracts. It follows that the time and resources that you unconsciously and habitually waste, while doing what you do to earn money, is building a subconscious barrier, by way of your belief pattern, preventing you from drawing money to you. If your actions express lack of interest with all the resources available for you to make or save money, then the resulting impression on your subconscious will cause you to overlook golden opportunities and hidden assets, which do exist, in the belief that you don't want them.

This is in line with an immutable Universal Law. Aristotle referred to it as the Law of Expression. What ever you express, in your actions, will be impressed into your deep-rooted beliefs; and what ever you impress, in your dominant thoughts, will be expressed in your life. If you squeeze an orange its juice will come to the surface. If you marinate it in wine, the wine, absorbed by the orange, will flavour the juice. Similarly, your absorbing actions on how you treat your existing wealth, whatever amount or form that resource currently takes, will inevitably and adversely affect your future prosperity. For this reason it is important to look at ways to simplify your work life as what you do to earn money must be able to net you what is available for you.

The combined promises of: Living on less than you earn and wisely investing the saving, must spring from the foundation you have to work with first. With a cluttered belief pattern and values of mindless consumerism based on misguided security and escapism, how can an increased flow of monetary energy come to you? It will only flow to that consciousness that impressly and expressly declares: ready to receive.

UNTANGLING YOUR NETS

The fact is that no amount of money in the world will make you comfortable if you are not comfortable with yourself. If your life is full of clutter, whether it be scarcity attitude clutter, obligation clutter, guilt clutter or just clutter then it will be difficult to see the wood for the trees. Most people view money as an expression of survival, getting by, rather than its true expression of freedom.

A fundamental belief pattern that is involved in survival mode will literally push money and abundance away from you. That is why the key is to see what money you have first, what you have earned and what you let through your fingers and allow to stand idle. Even a little amount of money helps to dampen down the debilitating emotions that generate the scarcity mentality.

The very fact you have some money is an affirmation that you are able to create it and can do it again in the future. It is only the amount that your deep-rooted and misguided beliefs will not accept. The rich get richer because of the overriding emotional release they experience from having wealth. Of course, it is easier to have an abundance mentality when you have wealth, but it does start in the mind first. Understand that wherever you are is the 'right' place at the 'right' time because your state of consciousness has made it so.

Your outer world is an expression of your inner world, and your inner level rests at the perpetual state your beliefs allow it to. So, when in concert with your beliefs of 'not so good,' you see all around you 'not so good,' this endorses your viewpoint. If you see the world through the lens of a scarcity mentality, and it is 'poor' you take on the hue of its infinite poverty. Conversely if you see your world as abundant, even if it is not currently so, it becomes so. It is difficult to detach yourself, however, from the survival anxiety created by your mind, when your work arena is junked with stuff.

Earlier the point was made that a good portion of your income may be going on the 'necessary' accoutrements considered essential for your work. Now consider how much you fully utilise this stuff, and if it has provided added value to your work. In this way you will begin to recognise whether it was your ego that persuaded you to have it, because everyone else had one, because the marketing of it convinced you or because it was vital to your work and has proved to serve you purposefully.

HAVE YOU BECOME A SLAVE TO 'TIME MANAGEMENT?

Have you insidiously evolved from a simple to-do list to executive leather-bound fold-out desk top time management system with spread-sheets for your daily schedule? Before moving up to your electronic organiser did you regularly engage in the numerous and multi-purpose tabulated sections for goals, projects, priorities, strategies, decisions, forward planners, backward planners, overview planners, expense summaries, personal information, interpersonal communications and daily, weekly, monthly and yearly calendars? Not forgetting the priority management overflow chart. If you did not go on a special course to learn how to use it efficiently did you study the instructions and keep to the required commitment of spending at least 30 minutes each day to evaluate progress, check off completed items, and transfer unfinished business to the next day's two page spread?

Did you, again before spending hours loading your electronic organiser, lump this 3 kilo time saving tool around with you from meeting to meeting in case you came up with a brilliant idea, or remembered to insert something to your project planning tabulation? Did it, or does it simplify your life or complicate it? The world's richest man, Bill Gates, won't have one, but then he doesn't even have a secretary.

The most successfully organised people have simplified their lives in order that they can focus on what they are good at. They do not allow their lives to be compartmentalised and structured to the point that the tail is wagging the dog. They concentrate on what they know and what works for them and do not allow the lure of activity to take them beyond what is productive yet comfortable and controllable.

Has your 3 kilo weight been replaced with another that you carry around in its own case? Are you in control of your computer or does it run your life? If you forget it, are you at sea suddenly, or can you still perform without it? The point is that are you master of your time and your productivity, or is your activity a complicated procrastination for focusing on what you really could be doing. The classic small 9cm x 15cm pocket diary way and simple daily to-do list may simplify your life in such a way that you can see the wood for the trees and actually achieve more. The main point is that if you're controlled by your time-management system, or any process for that matter, maybe it's time to look at how you can change it so that you control it instead.

ORGANISED

The idea of a time system does follow a sound principle: that of being organised. It is important to be organised, but its fundamental practice can get out of hand. When it becomes the priority rather than a useful tool it does actually become a form of procrastination actually distracting you from what is your main objective. Ask yourself do you have an ultimate objective? If not, then all your progress may be taking you in a different direction ~ a wrong one. Have you got your work priorities in order, particularly the general coming and going of the mountain of printed material that passes into your hands?

Do you have stacks of reading material such as magazines, journals, articles, catalogues and junk mail in files that you haven't read for months? Once you put a piece of paper away or file it, do you have trouble finding it again? Do you find it difficult to put things away because your filing cabinets are full? Is you work area clear? Is your desk a clutter most of the time? Without attention to getting and staying organised you will find it nigh impossible to simplify your life. And if that is what your consciousness is expressing just think what 'impression' you are making on it in your inner world.

You must make a commitment to yourself to address your work environment once and for all. If not, paper pushing will take over your life as you constantly handle and re-handle the piles of paper that the information age insists you take notice of. Regardless of whether you work out of an office or home begin by clearing the decks. Your desk top is a work area, not a storage area. Only have papers that you are currently working on.

Go through your filing system and clear out what is obsolete. If in doubt box up the cleared out items in an orderly fashion and store although you will find that what you remove will provide you with ample future room. A file does not require every letter, just the essence of the transaction. Alternatively invest in a scanner and place storage information on computer disc. The rule is file don't pile. Set aside ten minutes at the end of the day to keep on top of this important chore. Don't just move things around as this accomplishes nothing.

FISH BITS AND PIECES

Apparently one survey on the way people work revealed that people add to disorder by compulsively making notes on numerous bits of paper and notepads. More time is spent looking for the note, rewriting the note or moving the note contents from pad to pad, than is spent making the call or doing the thing that the note specified in the first place. Keep a large day to day diary on your desk and record in it every note, every call, every remembered thing to do, every idea that flashes to you. This stays on your desk, so cannot be lost, and is big enough to take everything you have to remind yourself to do as well as your doodles. More importantly you can write your tomorrow's to-do list periodically during the day taking the time at the end of each day to add to them and prioritise them in order of importance. At the same time correspondingly fill in your pocket book diary in the event you are away from the office. Make certain all messages are put into this desk diary with full details, even if you receive the message during your absence.

These simple procedures once again keep you on top of your work and ensure you are the master of your 'load' and not its slave. Even if you lose your small diary, everything is recorded back at the work-station. If you prefer to be electronic, follow the same principles so that at the end of each day the FISH rule of: Finish In Simplified Harmony, applies.

WHERE'S THAT NUMBER AND THIS PEN DOESN'T WORK

On sorting out your desk drawers are they full of others' business cards, telephone numbers, and unworkable, but smart, pens? When you suddenly have the idea to contact someone, relevant to an idea you have, do you have to trawl through all the cards each time. And why is it that whenever you want to leave a message with someone the message-taker's pen has either disappeared or refused to work? Business cards are like socks in the home. You start out with several pairs only to shortly end up with unmatching pairs all over the place.

Your database of contacts is one of your most valuable assets. Getting on in business is not about who you know or what you know. It is about what you do with what you know with who you know. And, if figuratively speaking, everyone you have ever met ends up stuck in a dark, messy drawer along with pens that don't work, it says a lot about your understanding and intentions to build future business relationships. The subliminal message is clear: don't bother to write to this person, who has bothered to give you this card, unless of course they are useful to you. John D. Rockefeller, history's biggest billionaire, kept every business card in an orderly fashion and referred to his network of contacts that he developed over 40 years as his biggest asset. President George Bush developed the habit of replying to everyone's card he received. Every night he would spend time writing letters building strong relationships.

Put all your cards in order. Those you consider relevant if you like. To test whether you need the others, throw them away. If within a week you suddenly find that one of them was important after all because of an idea you've had, or information you have received, this will cause you to record all names on to your database card or computer system in future. When you have recorded all names and addresses throw the card out. Then record them on a weekly basis.

As for your pens, pick the best working six pens and throw the rest out. The rest of the stuff in the draws should be easier to sort or throw. Cleared drawers means you can store your pending work each evening. Importantly make a mental note as to the amount of time and money you have spent in buying the junk in the drawers, previously sorting them out, and the lost earning potential by not following through the opportunities that the contact cards may have offered.

The great wisdom literature was written by individuals who had one pen and a bottle of ink. They were not distracted from their work by deciding on which pen to use, or finding one that worked. Remember Einstein's suits. They succeeded because their singlemindedness was not attacked by pointless distraction. The card and pen exercise is to bring to your attention how much of your time spent on unorganised trivia will dissipate your energy and focus.

THE BIGGEST WEIGHT OF ALL

Organise yourself into daily and weekly duties with regard to dealing with paperwork and paying bills. Often more reactive energy goes in finding ways around paying a bill than in proactive energy earning more to not even think about how to pay them. The biggest weight of all in business is usually cash-flow. If you make it a goal to organise your financial affairs so that you pay every bill that crosses your desk within seven days the psychological effect it has on your well-being is enormous.

Take a moment to consider briefly all the money you owe. Notice your emotional and mental state. Now imagine that you do not owe anyone a single penny. That all your accounts are fully up to date and you are not beholden to any other individual. Notice now how your emotional and mental state feels. In a word it feels a sense of freedom. And it is only in that sense of freedom that you can move forward in a way that literally attracts wealth to you.

Even though it may take some time to clear your current backlog of outstanding bills, if you commit yourself to not incurring any future ones associated with clutter, escapism or 'I wants,' and make it a priority to get yourself up to date, your growing sense of self-worth will benefit in every way. Clearing out the clutter throughout your work environment will remind you to ensure that only 100 per cent satisfaction should be received from any money you spend.

Everytime you spend money remember to enter it in your cash book. Put all the receipts in one dedicated box, together with incoming bills, and address them on a weekly basis by entering them into your books, paying them or marking them for payment at the due date, as appropriate.

DON'T GET HOOKED ON THE SYSTEM

Almost every company's account system is set up for payment in 30 days, though only a very small percentage ever stick to it. Too many, particularly the large ones, who are supposedly meant to be setting an example, show disrespect to suppliers through delayed payment. The excuse of 'the computer's down' and 'it's in the post' roll off the tongue so easily because it has become the norm. Many small businesses justify their own late payments because of the practice being dealt to them. The firm principle to follow is that any business should look to grow on its own merits of service, product and integrity and should not be at the mercy of another business's whim, cash shortage or computer quirk.

Too often businesses allow themselves to be sucked into compromising their business with the attraction of the 'big' customer. In doing so they effectively compromise the service and integrity they provide to their other customers. The true essence of business is to serve others and receive profit as the applause for that service. For it is only through service to others, real service, that your business will grow. It is not to survive by ducking and diving while hoping for the next big order.

When you pay your bills ahead of time you are certainly noticed and are almost certainly assured of improved terms and discounts. It may mean slower growth at first but infinite patience will always bring immediate results. It is no coincidence that 95 out of 100 businesses do not survive a period longer than just 60 months. Most have wanted to run before they can walk and not yet understood that cash-flow starts and ends with their actions.

COD RULES OK

When a business first starts it has to confine itself to the rule of COD. Without established creditworthiness, accounts or track record, it cannot get an overdraft or credit, so it has to pay Cash On Delivery. Can you imagine the health of the economy if every business continued to follow such a method, as part of their ethos. The cost of those businesses that do not succeed runs into billions. A post-mortem on most always reveals that cash-flow is the culprit. But how can it be? If the system is not working is it not a sounder principle to look at the system producer first in order to improve the system? Of course it is. Which is why every truly successful big fish was once a small fish who experienced failure.

ARE YOU SWALLOWING YOUR OWN BAIT?

Consider once more your current outgoings. Are they really essential for your income. Do they genuinely help you build your income or have they become just an overhead to service by habit? Would the money be better employed or invested elsewhere? Regularly reviewing your expenses, overheads and doing your accounts, regardless how small or insignificant you consider them to be, has the effect of bringing yourself to heel. The adage of 'out of sight, out of mind' can be dangerously true of your finances. If you leave it too long before you assess what you are doing to them, it may be too late. Going out for dinner or spending money on something you cannot afford when you have outstanding bills to be paid is actually playing with fire as far as your income is concerned.

Whether you are in employment or have your own business the same frame of reference should apply. Whatever you do to earn income you are effectively self-employed. Having a self-employed mentality requires you to be personally responsible, accountable to yourself and taking ownership of what you are required to do. Those with this mentality rise through the ranks because they are proactive and not reactive ~ because they embrace the maxim of: if it's to be, it's up to me. The reactive mentality of : don't do more than you're paid for; ask no questions and seek to take the credit, adhere to the maxim of: What's in it for me?

Being employed by another does not require you to divulge yourself of being personally responsible for your finances: how you earn your income and what you do with it. Following the principles in this book will lead you to financial independence while simplifying your life regardless of your employment details. These principles have led business owners netting £10,000 a year to become financially independent, increase their income dramatically and continue to do so. Conversely, non-compliance of these principles leads many corporate employees netting £100,000 a year to be continually anxious about how to meet their outgoings and to be completely dependent on external forces.

Further principles throughout this book will explain how you can increase your income continually, as it is important to be able to choose and bait our own hook in life. For now it is worth reiterating that you have to be master of what supports you first, in order to build the foundation to bear the fruit of your future growth.

UNDERSTANDING YOUR BUOYANCY

What is the purpose of your work? Why do you do what you do to earn money? What is it that motivates you to get out of bed five days a week to go out and earn money? We have come a long way since the time prior to the industrial revolution when our ancestors worked for a small portion of the day and enjoyed the pleasure of 'playing' the rest of the time. For the Greeks, leisure was the highest good, the essence of freedom. It was a time for self-development, learning and higher pursuits. Yet here we are with the supposed benefit of several thousand years of civilised growth, unable to relax and enjoy our leisure.

During the past 100 years we have unconsciously equated getting paid with work to the point that if we are not collecting income we cannot be working, we must be just playing, a frivolous pastime that serves no real purpose. The real problem with work is that we have confused it with how we are paid. Paid employment is just one activity among many of our other purposeful activities that fulfil our needs for stimulation, recognition, growth and contribution.

Our fulfilment does not actually lie in our jobs, but in the whole picture of our lives, in our inner sense of what life is about, our connectedness with others and our yearning for meaning and purpose. Understanding what makes us feel elated and buoyant in our lives means recognising that it is not what we do that is important, but what we have the potential to become when the restraining ropes, that hold us to the *needs* to earn income, are severed.

Most people view money as a necessity for survival, something that is required to get by in life. It is seldom viewed as an element for growth, something that provides the freedom to get on in life, a medium we exchange our life energy for. As a result of this its value is misguidedly measured against external definitions rather than what we invest our life energy in. How much we value ourselves is in direct proportion to how buoyant we are throughout life. Keeping your head just above water does not reflect a healthy buoyancy.

The degree to which you respect your self-worth is in direct proportion to how you treat your working environment and the income that comes to you. You are at this moment the sum total of everything you have ever done in your life to this point. Without addressing the way you view money and the way you earn and spend it, your level of buoyancy will not improve. This means looking at your motives for what you do and not just your moves.

Without understanding your motives for why you do what you do, you will create only short term relief from the continual raising your head above the surface. Prioritised to-do lists are the right moves but they are not your life. They are simply navigators whose purpose is to help your progress. They are not dictators to which you become a slave. It is your guiding motives that are the ultimate reason for how you feel about yourself and your subsequent self-worth.

Without a reason for what you do, striving for wealth is exhausting and does not bringing lasting financial independence. Similarly striving for happiness does not work, as happiness is a moment to moment experience. Having a specific mission, consistent values and measurable goals are important factors in developing your internal sense of worth, esteem and buoyancy.

If you are not certain about the keys essential to releasing your potential through personal development take the time to read *Born To Succeed* or similar self-help books. At this point, though, try to accept that you and you alone are solely responsible for the amount of money that you spend throughout your life. And as well as that, and this is the big one to swallow, you are also the only person responsible for the amount of money you earn and believe you are capable of earning.

7 ▪ Streamlining your Lifestyle and Health

Give a fish health and a course to steer and it'll never stop to trouble about whether it's happy or not.
With apologies to George Bernard Shaw

"DO YOU SWALLOW *food accidentally?*", *the Sturgeon asked the Lump Fish who had visited him in the hope of reducing his excess weight.*

"*What do your mean?*", *the Lump Fish replied indignantly.* "*It's hardly my fault. I'm just prone to putting on weight. I've tried every diet but they don't seem to work, I generally end up putting on more weight than I have lost. I want you to just remove my fat surgically. I'm so busy and I just can't afford the time to keep worrying about my health. You're the expert, can't you just sort my problem?*"

"*Unless we identify the source of your weight,*" *the Sturgeon persisted,* "*it will be pointless just cutting away the fat to sort out your problem. If you are not concerned about what, or how much, you are eating then you might as well be swallowing food by accident."*

A good state of health is the fundamental key to a happy life, yet, amazingly, its priority is placed down the scale after financial and material states. And bearing in mind the usual financial and material states of the majority of retired people this does not bode well for good health. The whirlpool of worry affecting health and subsequently your health problems making you worry is actually a ridiculously self-induced position to put one's self in. It's also an expensive one.

Billions and billions are spent every year on the countless 'wonder-diets', guaranteed to carve out the new you. The topical conversation of 'how many *pounds* you have lost' is ironically apt. You spend money to lose the weight that came about from the money you spent literally building it. You spend more money on exercise equipment you don't use, on more 'elixirs' that don't *seem* to work, and then on drugs or operations to sort out the inevitable results of ill health and any adverse side effects. Yes, *losing pounds* is very apt indeed!

Removing the clutter from your arteries is obviously significantly more important than removing the clutter from your home and work, although they are interrelated. Their success follows the same principle of simplifying complex processes. The more you eat the less you live and the less you eat the more you live. Paradoxically this translates to: the longer you live the more you can eat. So if you like food then understand that you will only eat more by literally eating less.

Certainly it is worth investing in books and courses to assist in health improvement but first and foremost is an acceptance of your own duty. That you are responsible for your own health. Regardless of your eating habits, sleeping habits, drinking habits, smoking habits, slouching habits, or whatever habits, their moderation or indulgence is down to you. Taking the time to listen to your own common sense, intuitive guidance or the blatant resulting side-effects you carry around with you, are just three of the many personal pointers that constantly serve to remind you of what you are doing to yourself. Sadly the majority do not heed any pointers or suggestions and continue to lose countless pounds from both their wallet and weight, which remain inextricably linked.

What is common-sense, of course, is seldom common practice and what is common practice has become uncommonly complicated. Getting and staying healthy is actually simple and not time consuming but it does involve blowing apart certain misguided beliefs and ending practices that are not necessary.

Lump Fish had finally 'promised' himself to do something about his health. He wanted to lose weight and be fit and healthy and so, right after the coming festive season he decided to make a start. There was little point in starting this side of Christmas as it was only a couple of weeks away and he wanted to 'enjoy' himself. Following his new resolution he signed up at a local health and fitness centre. It was more expensive than he had thought it would be and meant committing to a 3, 6 or 12 month plan. There was a New Year Member's offer that included a free fitness assessment whereupon he would receive his personalised routine, but he also managed to negotiate a six month plan into a three month plan. He was excited as he imagined the result of soon looking like a lean mean fighting machine with a herring bone mid-driff.

The first week he decided to give it his all and intensely went almost every night after work. Gosh it was harder than he thought it would be, especially as the fitness test had encouraged him that he was not in bad shape for his age. And making an impression with those young sprats was even harder. He couldn't for the life of him understand why they went anyway as they were already fit and looked great. Last night he didn't finish his routine as he was a bit stiff from over doing the previous session although he promised himself he would make it up.

"I didn't think I would be this busy so quickly in the year," he said to himself. It was annoying about that appointment coming up as it was only the third week and it was the second time he had been prevented from going to the centre. No matter he was feeling better and had lost some of the weight he had wanted. He would just have to continue to watch what he ate.

Having not been to the centre for a month now he was pleased to learn from a colleague that he too had given 'this fitness thing' a go, but who wanted to be scrawny and brawny anyway? They agreed that these centres were not all they were made up to be and you had to be fanatical to go. Mind you he still had to do something about his weight. Perhaps he would make an appointment with that Sturgeon his colleague had mentioned?

TEN COMMON TRAITS

Conditioned by the 'have it now' factor, we set ourselves unrealistic expectations. When we decide to be fit we want it to be over and done with as soon as possible. If we do not get what we want quickly we look to blame the very thing we had hoped would be the vehicle to give us what we demanded. Lump Fish's outcome was spawned because he allowed himself to flow with ten common traits.

1. His *'promise'* was not sustained by his *personal integrity*. Going from zero exercise to Olympic runner in 90 days is not possible as physical endurance and strength can only be built one step at a time for as long as it takes. Similarly, personal integrity can only be built by making and keeping lots of small promises before the habit of keeping larger promises is acquired. If he had resolved to become healthier by starting

at a pace he was comfortable with he would have found it easier to keep his promise and build on them. For example: beginning with a tiny promise of taking a weekly walk for ten minutes is achievable. Following this success with two walks a week and then a daily walk is a natural progression as psychological and physiological stamina grows. On this foundation greater promises and consequential bigger demands can be kept. This leads on to the second trait.

2. Taking a daily brisk walk for 20 minutes will make you very fit but fitness must not be confused with health. They are not the same. The *perception* of Lump Fish, was that *fit and healthy* were. The same is true of how we perceive them. As a result of this we experience the stress and frustration of zealously working out while still having weight clinging to those areas we want to remove the most. Those who in time become obsessed with exercise in the belief that they are becoming healthier end up more fatigued, more frustrated and more stressed out. Achieving fitness at the expense of your health is not using your common sense. The balance of being healthy and fit is as important as the balance between your savings and income. The best way to achieve this is the natural way and this is explained later on this chapter.

3. The 'little point in starting' was plain *procrastination* by Lump Fish. When something is important then there is no better time than the present to start it. Delaying something has the adverse effect of making it a bigger task than it actually is. Furthermore to delay creates an association of something that will not be enjoyable. To keep putting off something as you want to '*enjoy*' yourself first, sends the wrong signals to your inner health bank balance.

4. The next trait was that Lump Fish sought to *negotiate* or *compromise* his health programme. The paradox of the faster you push, the slower you move holds true. An old, yet adapted, Zen story illustrates this. A young swordfish who wanted to be a great fighter eagerly sought out a renowned sword Master and asked how long it would take for him to learn great swordfish skills.

"Ten years perhaps," replied the Master. Clearly impatient for a result, the student inquired how long it would take if he worked exceptionally hard.

"In that case, it will probably take 20 years," replied the Master. Frustrated at what he was hearing the student asked: "Look , I'm willing to suffer any kind of hardship and sacrifice I just want to learn in the shortest time possible." "In that case," the Master replied, you'll have to study with me for 30 years."

5. In concert with the above trait was that Lump Fish was only concerned with the *result* of his actions. We cannot negotiate the time period to attain health as we have no control over the result only over the actual process. The expression of 'no pain, no gain', is not a natural way for a healthy life. Building physical strength follows the same principle that crops in the soil follow. In the natural environment and nurtured with the good nutrients they come to harvest at the right time. The process is continuous, not occasional, fitted in or to suit. It is, of course, important to visualise the outcome of what you want to achieve but this must be balanced with the daily action towards the visualised outcome. Although the accomplished Yogi may be able to build the physical being through his mental actions, his daily procedures are always consistent with developing that ability.

6. To gain the instant result Lump Fish *intensely* worked at his routine. The motivation required for his over indulgence was difficult to maintain and inevitably proved impossible to sustain. Being too intense without the foundation of personal integrity and attention to process will not prevail in any situation be it health, relationships or business. And inevitably leads to:

7. The 'didn't finish' syndrome which is the precursor to generally *quitting*. When the understanding and desire is not fully instilled, what was initially considered a priority soon begins to wane. Other priorities in the form of being busy and other appointments soon take precedence once more as through habit we continue to act in that manner that rests most comfortably with us. This, in turn, leads to:

8. *Rationalising* why something was perhaps not such a good idea after all. Our comfort zone understands us better than anyone else and knows just how to strike at our Achilles Heel. It allows us to find reasons why we can't do something, ignoring the common-sense pleas of why we can do it. It forces us to conform to the pattern we have been conditioned to believe is right for us even if it is unerringly leading us towards failure.

'To learn from a colleague' that he, too, was of a like mind provides the rational support required in this case for Lump Fish to:

9. Seek the *justification* for his actions on quitting his health routine by agreeing with his colleague that they were not 'fanatical' and that there must be:

10. Another *alternative* to attain better health and fitness more suited to his time frame and lifestyle. Metaphorically making an 'appointment with that Sturgeon' similarly to Lump Fish is simply putting a broken leg in plaster without setting the bone first. Quick-fix alternatives are not the secret to getting your life in order and enjoying a healthy lifestyle.

STROKES FOR IMPROVING YOUR MOTION AND BALANCE

With the energy of salmon returning to the spawning pools, so many of us chase after an externally suggested solution when the real secrets for healthy living are present inside all of us. Here are offered the alternatives that really do lead to a healthy lifestyle. Your body and your mental, physical and emotional states are affected by what you eat. We are what we eat.

Without the power of choice exclusive to humans, animals in the wild do not get bigger than they are intended to. Domesticated animals often get overweight and ill, as the size of that specific animal health care industry illustrates. Does this mean that how we live our own lives influences those close to us? Of course it does. It also influences the size of the daily multi-million pound health-care budget required to sustain our personal habits of choosing to live with indulgence and extravagance rather than temperance and moderation. It is important to use our unique power of choice for our benefit, not our detriment.

Choosing to develop new strokes not only keeps our bodily health in balance but it also directly affects the health of our bank balance. The simple change, for example, of not food shopping when you are tired, hungry or thirsty, together with a specific understanding of what it is that you want to eat has a profound effect on both. You know from your own experience that when you shop without a list you always end up spending more than you anticipated on things that do not provide 100 per cent satisfaction or value. Usually the subtle persuasion of advertising works on you to come home with items you did not intend to purchase.

This chapter does not seek to advise what foods, drinks and nutrients you should or should not eat. There are many excellent fundamental guides available for that. What it does seek to reiterate, though, are key pointers that, when followed, will lead you to improve the health of your body and income.

FIRST : THE CAT FISH RULE

The three keys essential to master balance in these two interrelated areas are: Consumption, Activity and Tranquillity.

These three factors are also interrelated in the respect that to the degree you consume, are active, or at ease, will correspondingly affect the others. For example: eat too much or too little, and it is difficult to be active. Too much or too little rest makes you inactive, too much or too little activity makes you unable to rest. The body's natural system, when listened to and followed will balance these three factors. But it is seldom allowed to. The simple way to keep to your optimum weight is to allow your body's metabolism to do its job.

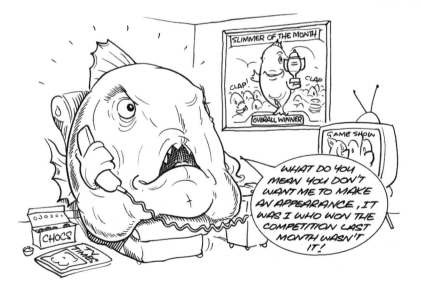

Diets serve only to confuse your metabolic rate. Repeat or yo-yo dieting slows it down causing your body to store more energy in the form of fat. That is why 95 per cent of all people who lose weight end up regaining it. You can literally diet yourself up in size. That is also why top diet companies do not publish their success rate. Consumption today is generally less in calories than the 1950s, but the proportion of fat in our diet has increased by 50 per cent while the level of activity has decreased. Couch-potato syndrome is part of the problem with over half of adults and primary school children not engaging in regular physical activity whatsoever.

There are two types of activity: aerobic and anaerobic. Aerobic means, literally, with oxygen, and refers to moderate exercise sustained over a period of time. When you activate your aerobic system, which encompasses the heart and lungs, with a moderate diet, activity and rest, you burn fat as your primary fuel. Conversely anaerobic means without oxygen and refers to exercises that produce short bursts of power.

Anaerobic exercise burns glycogen as its primary fuel, while causing the body to store fat. Today's stressful and demanding lifestyle compounded with short spurts of activity, causes metabolism to be continuously anaerobic. When levels of glycogen becomes excessively low, the anaerobically trained metabolism turns to blood sugar as its secondary source of fuel. This immediately robs you of your health and vitality while still building up reserves of fat.

Genetics plays a part in your body's ability to burn fat. Some are born with a higher aerobic level than others ~ those individuals who seem able to eat anything without ever gaining an ounce. But you can train your metabolism. Your body will not burn fat unless you train it to. You have to train it to burn fat not sugar. How? By simply taking regular daily walks! And that is brisk, yet comfortable walks, not leisurely strolls. Our modern, time-saving lifestyle has developed machines and systems to do everything previous generations actively did. Remote controls to elevators, drive-in fast food restaurants to sandwich deliveries, could almost have been specifically designed to help you save more calories than time.

A lunch hour is perfect for 20 minutes consumption, 20 minutes activity and 20 minutes tranquillity ~ literally body, mind and spirit rejuvenation. The reality is a quick ingest of highly calorific fast food which has been brought in while either continuing with work or anaerobically shopping. Think about your own lunch break? Do you take the opportunity to recharge the batteries in the areas of mind, body, spirit, or do you keep you keep telling yourself you should while loading yourself up with tasty escapism? Stroke one means start thinking CATnap by using your lunch-time as an opportunity to effectively streamline your lifestyle and health.

Regular exercise is important in your life. Every able-bodied person should be able, in time to build up to just 30 minutes of walking and stretching. The main thing is to ensure that you burn fat and not sugar. The simple test is that when you're exercising can you talk? This is aerobic. Or are you out of breath? This is anaerobic. Your breathing should be steady and audible, but not laboured. Your activity should be pleasurable though tiring. Don't start tomorrow, as it never comes, start today.

SECOND: BAIT

Walk down to the book shop or library and get a book on healthy eating, not dieting. Buy the one you feel suits you best. You make the decision. Every one knows the adage of: an apple a day keeps the doctor away, so make certain that your diet includes fruit. Nature in its infinite wisdom will always simplify the natural process of life. It fits the eater with the food. Look at your hands and teeth. Has nature designed them to pick and eat fruit? What do you think, instinctively?

Look at your digestive system. Has nature designed it to cope with what you may be currently passing through it? Let your intuitive reasoning help you along? It is important to do what you are comfortable with doing. But the key word is comfortable. Is your body comfortable with how you treat it? Or is it uncomfortably displaying the evidence and symptoms of swallowing the wrong bait?

Make certain you begin to fish for the new you with the correct bait or you might end up catching something that does not rest comfortably. Simplify your eating habits ~ you already know that you should, but start right now by just taking one week at a time.

Don't go the other way with a *quick-fix intensity*! Allow your body to adjust and your mind to accept week by week by week until the habit comes about. See your body as the temple of your spirit as this will help to build the desire for a healthier lifestyle.

THIRD: FISH DISCOVER WATER LAST

The most widely consumed cold liquids, in order of preference are coffee, sodas, diet drinks, milk, alcoholic beverages, carbonated fruit drinks and teas. If you fall into the 75 per cent of the population that is at least 20 per cent overweight and did nothing more than substitute your choice for water you would reduce to your optimum weight over the next year ~ 3 per cent of our body would reduce to a few minerals, the rest is water. It is essential to us yet we *discover it last*. Unfortunately the taste of tap water is not good and bottle water is more expensive than petrol, but it is still cheaper than most bought drinks and investing in a good water filter can eliminate the chlorinated taste from water.

Again begin moderately by cutting out caffeinated drinks such as carbonated sodas, coffee and tea ~ are addictive and as such will sometimes cause severe withdrawal symptoms including headaches, depression and nausea.

FOURTH: START TO BREATHE AND RELAX

Just for a moment take a few moments to breathe in really deeply through your nose, hold it for a few seconds and then breathe out slowly through your mouth. Do this four times. Feel better? Breathing properly actually accelerates your body's essential cleansing via your lymph system by over 1,000 per cent. Yes that's 1,000 per cent. What is your lymph system? Put simply it is your body's sewage system and you have four times more lymph than you do blood. Your heart pumps your blood and your breathing moves your lymph. Yet, amazingly, people do not know how to breathe properly. Most have lost the art, except smokers who have to breathe deeply to inhale smoke. More time is spent on curing malignant, cancerous and toxic oxygen starved cells than preventing their development simply by breathing properly. How's that for a crazy world?

The quality of your health is really the quality of your cells. They are kept healthier by enjoying a fully oxygenated system. Therefore, effective breathing has to be a priority in your life. Try *not* breathing. If you can only do it for less than 30 seconds think how starved your lymph system might be.

Learn how to breathe properly. Take a yoga course that involves stretching and breathing. The principles of hatha (physical) yoga have been practised for centuries because of the increased vitality, reduced fatigue, improved efficiency, enhanced concentration, and the serenity and peace of mind they generate. Yoga can be learned by all people of all ages and it will strengthen, firm, tone and shape your body, in addition to relaxing you and assisting your lymph system.

To start try this. At least 3 times a day, stop and take 10 deep breaths. Start deep in your abdomen. Breathe in through your nose for 4 seconds, hold for up to 16 seconds and then breathe out very slowly, for 8 seconds, through your mouth. If you find it difficult to breathe with your abdomen, initially lie on the floor and put your hand on your stomach. Try to breathe so that you can feel your abdomen rise first, then your chest. Make this a part of your life as there is no food, vitamin pill or drug in the world that can do for you what an excellent breathing pattern can do. You will find in time that you are breathing better, your posture is better and that you generally have more vitality.

LOTS OF LITTLE EFFECTIVE STROKES

Learn to meditate. This will give you more time and you will get more done. Why? Because meditating will give you a new understanding of your life, and will help you get clear on exactly how you want to live your life.

● Learn to be yourself. Don't assume a façade of pretence for someone else's needs. You complicate your life and waste your energy by pretending to be someone other than you are.

● Learn to trust your intuition. Ask yourself if your lifestyle has become so hectic that you have forgotten to listen to what your intuition sounds like, let alone pay attention to it. Do you listen instead to a conditioned rationale?

- Learn to do better what you are good at and eliminate what you find difficult. You will only become outstanding at that which comes naturally to you. Ask yourself how much of your energy is spent at those things you will never excel at.

- Learn to change yourself, not others. Why convince yourself you must have the endorsement of others for how you now choose to live your life? The best way to influence is by example.

- Learn to do one thing at a time. This makes solid sense. So concentrate on what you want to do.

- Learn to say no. It's your life and both your life and relationships improve when you learn this skill.

- Finally, learn to take time out for yourself and think. Get up an hour earlier, spend a day a month in solitude, go off to a retreat once a year ~ it's good for the soul. Streamlining your lifestyle and health can only be a personal choice. There is no stronger soul to direct you than that of your own and uncluttering your mind and body is as essential as the uncluttering of your home and work. It needs to be done before you can literally see the wood for the trees. In this way you begin to experience the paradox of being able to refocus on broader horizons. Recognising opportunities that you have overlooked before but that nonetheless exist is the key to your continued growth and development in life.

Part Three

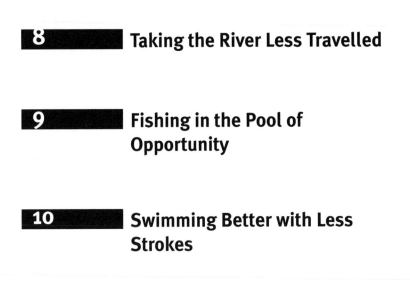

8 ■ Taking The River Less Travelled

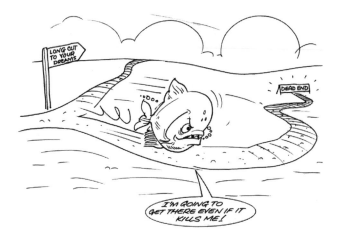

What is the use of running when you are on the wrong road?
Proverb

PETE PIRANHA *could not get over the feeling of exhilaration his growing sense of new found freedom gave him. Since clearing the trivia from his life, he did not seem so weighed down, both physically and mentally. He literally felt a whole lot lighter and now found it considerably easier to focus on what he wanted to accomplish during the rest of his life.*

The process of simplifying his life had brought with it a realisation. All you really have in life is time. No fish knew exactly how much you had, but how you decided to spend it, where you spend it and with whom, was really up to you. That's what freedom is. And seeking a false sense of security while wasting your time and money on stuff that you didn't really value or need, was just relinquishing your freedom.

*The incredible thing was that he could think clearer.
Simplifying his external world had actually led to a greater
clarity in his inner world. His continual frustration at not
having enough money, or enough orders, or enough of stuff
had clouded so many things for him. As the discipline to
spend less, save more, invest the difference and ensure 100
per cent satisfaction for anything spent, had grown his
frustration had been replaced with a confidence. A
confidence growing inside him just from being his own fish.*

*Just the other day he had decided to swim a route he had
not taken before. Perhaps it was because he had more time
now, although he certainly got more of the right things done
than he ever had before, that he had decided to take this
route. He had to admit that he was fearful at first as he
turned off the boiling freeway, it was so murky on the edges
from all the disturbance thrown up. It was only because of
his new found sense of freedom that he felt like breaking
from the herd for a change and had spontaneously flipped off
the freeway. As he wondered why it was called a freeway,
when every morning it was at a standstill, the murkiness
suddenly cleared. Free Way. At that moment he knew what
he wanted to do.*

Strangely the hardest decisions to be made in life are the
ones that result in making us the most comfortable ~ in the
long term. The very process of working towards deciding to
do what we really want to do, do our own thing, not be
beholden to others and experience the freedom and power of
personal choice, follows a path full of self-imposed
impediments. Top of the list are usually guilt and

conditioning that manifest themselves as 'I should, I ought' or 'there was no choice'. The fact is that wherever we find ourselves is because of either previous choice or non-choice.

Perhaps the number one choice that certainly most individuals, as well as an amazing amount of businesses make, is to *not* decide on an ultimate objective. The consequence is that many lives, and businesses, are run by default. In the same way that a chosen program set by default on a computer will influence all future work, the outcome in your life will be influenced by your thinking mode. Wherever you are at is because of the default setting you have allowed yourself to operate under. It is as simple as that.

'Better the devil we know than the devil we don't know' too often dictates our lives to the point that we compromise the development of our full potential. It is only when we are forced to re-evaluate, because of a shock to our system, that we consider the 'unknown'. What will be your shock? Redundancy, divorce, illness, heart attack, nervous breakdown, loss or will it be a conscious processed and evaluated decision taken in those quiet moments of contemplation?

What will be your unknown? Will it be seeking to restore a status quo, replace a loss or reset back to 'normal' as quickly as possible? Or will it be seeking the opportunity to revisit those long-lost dreams and 'one-day I'll' aspirations that your inherent talents and strengths are able to make so achievable if only given the chance?

LEAVING THE RAPIDS

As simple as it may sound, taking one step at a time will always take you where you want to go, as long as you are certain of the direction you want to go. There is a wonderful feeling in choosing how you want to live your own life and then acting on your decisions. When you are committed to working towards a specific objective you are engaged in, the ultimate process of creating yourself through what you do is seen for what it really is ~ an adventure. The process of your life is the adventure, not the result.

Accidentally falling into rapids will spontaneously create the ultimate objective to escape them. Why? This is because your natural will to survive is triggered when the life-threatening strong currents take control of your destiny. If you find yourself unable to get out, the now surging adrenaline spawned by the Survival Will, creates a secondary objective: to survive within the situation it is caught.

In time you learn to swim and a further objective is created: to swim even more effectively. You learn to stay ahead of others who have also fallen into the rapids as they are perceived as a threat to your new found security of being a good swimmer. As external factors now require so much of your time and effort, just to keep your head above water, your mainland objective of developing your own path becomes increasingly distant.

Swimming in the rapids is an exhilarating adventure but the ability to get out of them can be a more fulfilling one. And fulfilling objectives are the keys to fully developing every area of our lives. Leaving the rapids is simply a metaphor for stopping work on the urgent busy-ness of your life and to start concentrating on the important business of your life. As a result of the nature of rapids, whirlpools are always created. Whirlpools will always suck you down and it takes enormously strong strokes to escape from their grasp.

Whirlpools are created in your life when there is a downward pulling force. Ask yourself. Do you feel as if you have a downward pulling force in your life? As if your energy is being drained from you, leaving you wondering where you're actually working towards? Could it be that you have become used to the rapids in your life to the point that any alternative actually now threatens the false sense of security your conditioned swimming skills have generated?

All the previous strokes that have required you to unclutter your life, simply by getting your house and spending affairs in order, are foundational to building the confidence and habit to establish and keep to your ultimate objective. All the energy, time, effort and money that you have previously put into trivia, escapism, unvalued commodities and non-saving elements, in the past have effectively reduced any focus you might have had. Certainly it is nigh impossible to decide, get and maintain focus when your life is full of just stuff. It's like having a cluttered desk before you start first thing in the morning. How can energy be focused on priorities when numerous 'things' are there to distract you.

Having made certain promises since reading this book, and taking definite decisions and actions you are now ready to make the move.

RE-INVENTING YOURSELF

The concept of choosing work that you want to do is based on the precept that your work is a reflection of who you are. Your work should be an area of great passion. It is irrelevant what your work is, how you do it, what you do it for, or whether you are an employee or employer so long as you enjoy it and it forms an important part of your life. Your work occupies a major part of your life and provides the opportunity to fully express yourself in a measurable way.

The freedom to choose one's work is a freedom lost to many as a 'rapid' society has deemed that anyone not seeking to join the scramble to make money is spiritless and lacking in ambition. Thinking has gone awry. The desire to gain wealth is overshadowed by the fear of losing what has been gained and the obsession for more and more has led to the slavery to consumption and possession. The paradoxical result is that the fiercest and most well-fed piranhas have become the hungriest and unfulfilled.

Society's most dominant behaviours will always seek to ensure acceptance as the norm. The usual practice becomes a false principle and the true principle becomes lost. Society's cry of 'Its a matter of principle' is seldom the truth. The reality is that there is rarely a Universal Principle involved.

A principle is just conveniently created to protect a perceived loss, benefit or simply to 'teach' someone a lesson for doing something out of the accepted norm. There can be only one answer, and that must be the one that closely adheres to the principle of being true to yourself and having the courage of your own convictions based on established priorities and fundamental values.

Our capacity to find ourselves is directly linked to losing ourselves in that thing that completely absorbs us ~ the love of a task before us. In that moment we learn an identity that lives both within and beyond us. The whole process of reducing the junk from our lives opens the way to changing the way we think, to reinventing ourselves.

GOOD FOR THE SOLE

Regardless of whether you work for yourself or another, operate singly or with a large organisation it is important to have a sole practitioner mind-set. You are self-employed, regardless of how you believe you are employed. It is not important where the money comes from or how you get paid, having a self-employed mentality is the only way forward for you. The employee mentality will always view the world differently to the employer mentality.

The classic them and us which exists at most work levels, structures and environments. The former will always consider that they work for another, the latter will always consider that they work with another. Just that simple but fundamental difference in thinking can have a major effect on your attitude, behaviour, relationships and material wealth. The former earns money, the latter makes money. What is your current mentality? Is it employee and scarcity or employer and abundant?

If you are brutally honest with yourself you will know the answer. To assist in your own questioning continue to ask yourself over the next 24 hours if you:

1. take personal responsibility for everything you do;
2. readily take full ownership of everything you have agreed to do;
3. fully accept any accountability regardless of the outcome;
4. deal with any money, no matter for what reason, as if it were your own;
5. deal with everyone as if they were your only customer.

Those who fully embrace the required mentality that being self-employed demands, be it on the shop-floor, the board room, the doorway, the classroom, the home, the holiday will most decidedly have the right thinking. Observe over the next seven days how often you qualify your responses either in a negative or non-decisive manner.

Consider if your comments to others are seeking power and credit but not responsibility and involvement. Being aware of how you react rather than respond will be able to confirm to you which mentality you currently operate under.

If you are genuinely experiencing difficulty in accepting the precept of being self-employed when for the past ten years you have always been employed, done what is expected of you to the full and been remunerated to the full then ask yourself who is ultimately responsible for you and your actions. Is it the person who pays you? The person who instructs you? The person who hires and fires you? The organisation behind all the decisions? No. It is you and only you.

Only you are responsible for you, where you live, what you do, and how you live.

EXPLORING NEW WATERS

Where you want to live is very often as important as what you want to do. A place will never be perfect of course but it's where your head and heart are that counts, not your body. Many of us have a dream of where we would like to live and work but rule it out because the idea of compromise has been so drummed into us that we don't believe we can have what we actually want. So, we either settle for something less or stay where we are.

It is worth giving yourself and your ideal place at least half a chance by considering the possibilities. Again, because of the expediency factor of wanting things that we have decided on immediately, insufficient planning and thought is taken. The estate agent is called in to value the house and, although notice may not be actually given, the work expressed is as if it has been. Hold it right there.

First allow yourself at least a 12 or 24-month time frame. Any move is not to be made to reduce your accumulated debts or provide more income. Your new way of thinking, living and commanding your spending and savings is for that. Where you live must be connected with what you want to be and do, if only to save on the commuting in order to provide you with more quality time to do it, or to be with the family more often.

It may be that you want to stay in the same career by either telecommuting, switching employers or going into business for yourself. It may be that you want to have a complete change of career and plan towards doing the work you have always considered doing. As your mind is continually relieved from its burden of ducking and diving, making ends meet or juggling everything in the air, it will be able to provide you with innovative solutions as to the way forward and to assist you to plan carefully.

Max Monkfish enjoyed his work as an engineer and he was rewarded well for what he did. During the past six months since he and his wife Miranda had been systematically reducing their expenditure and had actually started saving, he had found it easier to think about where they would really like to live and bring up their two children. It wasn't that he lived far from his employment, the main crux was that both he and Miranda did not feel comfortable where they lived. Both had been raised in the country and enjoyed walking.

Rather than take the usual holidays abroad, they both decided that over the next 12 months they would take regular week-end trips to Streamton. Their two week vacation really helped them to get to know the area very well.

The area was not so remote as they had originally thought and in fact was convenient to some major conurbations. The idea came to him that perhaps there was a way that he could generate new clientele for his existing employer in this area and be the field support engineer. Before making any proposals, however, he took several trips building up research and facts. He approached a few companies some of which indicated an interest. He then successfully received his employer's agreement to a 12 month trial period, after all it was an innovative idea by one of their specialists to increase new business so why not.

Several discussions with the local estate agents persuaded him to rent rather than buy. Both he and his wife considered it more prudent to not compromise their savings plan, so decided to attain a definite sale first before they made the move. Only when they had sold, would they then rent giving the time to find the right property and to confirm that this really was the place for them. They did not intend moving location again and wanted to be absolutely certain that they were in control and not circumstances.

"There was always the uncertainty that the new field position might not work out," said Max, "but I considered that it was no less secure than my existing position. Indeed some of my colleagues had been made redundant the previous year when a large order was withdrawn. The only security seemed to be one that generated opportunity. My proposals put me more in command of my future than I was previously and definitely the incentive and motivation to make it work!"

Their house took longer to sell than they would have liked, however. "On reflection it was good that it did," said Miranda, "as it not only tested our resolution to move, and if we were doing the right thing, it also allowed us the time to conclude the financial plan we had promised to stick to. When we did move, we did not owe anyone a cent and our savings were much greater than even I had imagined. Although we will shortly be committing ourselves once more at the time, we didn't even have a mortgage! And when we do commit ourselves we have planned to always pay a larger monthly payment than required, as owning our home is an important part of our ongoing plan."

Max Monkfish achieved a balance between where he wanted to live, what he wanted to do and what he was already rewarded for by thinking of how he could best serve both his company and clients. When you consider alternatives founded on working with a company, rather than for a company innovative ideas are spawned where everyone can win and grow. Contrary to popular belief companies do not like or even generally want to downsize as they can only grow through the joint efforts of everyone working with common purpose and shared values. Max took the time to clarify his priorities, establish what was important and plan proposals where he could serve himself through serving his company.

Many may not be so fortunate in relocating, although it has to be said that the outcome for Max and Miranda was brought about by their specific and proactive actions. Some will seek to move and not be able to stay with the same employer.

Pearl Perch knew where she wanted to move. She had also taken the time to evaluate all the possibilities and none of them would allow her to persuade her current employer to agree to her moving. She had suggested telecommuting, but was informed that it was not a policy under consideration, even though they were an electronics company. She also enjoyed her work. As a departmental manager she was good at what she did, was well remunerated and well liked. Her difficulty was that since her divorce she had been unable to afford the kind of property she wanted closer to work. Where she currently lived was fine apart from the fact that she spent too much of her time commuting.

There were other personal reasons why she wanted to move and this culminated in her seeking to switch employers. She decided that the key for her to do this would be to ask herself,

"What does the employer in the area I want to move to need that only I can provide?" What sets me apart from others equally qualified for the job?" Pearl made up her mind that the best way to persuade a future employer that she was a valuable asset to their business would be by demonstrating what a valuable asset she currently was to her present employer. A close friend and adviser said that this was not the way to go about things. It was best to keep quiet about it unless people did not approve of what see was doing and terminated her existing employment, in which case she would be without any income.

Since reducing clutter in her life she had promised herself to not replace it, and this included emotional clutter. Believing that honesty was the best course of action she approached both employers explaining that she enjoyed what she did and the success of her work was plain to see in her department. She further explained that the main reason she wanted to change employers was because of her desire to live in the new area.

People who know what they want and where they are going appeal to others because they appear intelligent, strong, confident, self-assured and sensible. In sharing her idea of how she wanted to live her life and how her work fitted into that picture, both employers were impressed. Her future employer, however, did not anticipate a vacancy for at least six months but promised to employ her when they did. Her current employer also agreed to keep her on for that period, even though she had shared her intention to leave, in order that she could train her replacement.

"The amazing, almost unthinkable thing is," Pearl reported some months into her new position, "that the two companies have now developed a strategic alliance together! Over the

last six months a good understanding and relationship has developed between certain elements of component production and sales."

TESTING THE WATER TO GO ON YOUR OWN

When Graham Rudd first learned that there would have to be inevitable redundancies over the next two years he immediately decided to anticipate the possibility of being one of them. He had heard the complacent tales of many fish who chose to do nothing until they were actually confronted with the reality of being jobless. Perhaps he was more conscious of taking advance action because of his cousin Paul's recent experience. It seemed that even though Paul had been given 18 months warning and even knew how much his redundancy package would be, he had adopted a 'let's wait and see attitude.' In the belief that something would turn up over such a long time, Paul had spent most of his time complaining that it wasn't fair and that some fish ought to be brought to account for it and why did it have to happen to him. After the time period had passed it was almost as if complacency compelled Paul to wait a further 12 months simply because his redundancy package would allow him to.

Graham was determined to turn his situation into an opportunity to go into business on his own account. An important part of his planning involved looking to his current employer as a future client. As a graphic designer he was good and understood the requirements of both his existing employer and their customers. There was another driver too, he no longer wanted to live in the city. He planned to persuade, and prove, to his employers that he would be even more creative working from his new home.

Over the next 12 months he and his family took the time to identify where they would like to live. They made all the necessary plans and he took the time to study the technology that would allow him to transmit his work from wherever he lived. He then volunteered to take early redundancy using the package to invest in the equipment that would allow him to continue to create, transmit and present his graphic work to his future clients. His company agreed to provide an initial twelve month consultancy agreement. He knew that he still had some way to go and would require further clients but he had overcome the biggest hurdles of deciding, making a start and overcoming securiti-itis. Indeed over the next 12 months he felt more secure and both his work and referrals had developed.

The important growth for *Graham Rudd* was that he had chosen to grasp the Damocles sword, which had been swung over his head and used it to carve out a path that had ultimately benefited both him and his employer. Telecommunications may have made it possible for many former city-type businesses to operate from anywhere in the country, but the key elements are establishing your priorities while fully utilising your greatest strengths. In this way you, and not circumstances, remain in control of your destiny.

Solicitors, accountants, doctors, dentists and similar professionals have often left their existing firms to start their own business in other parts of the country. Although some are able to receive referral work from former employers initially, many more build their own business by acquiring new clients in their new location.

As society, companies and individuals must inevitably prepare for a new de-jobbed world of work, increasing numbers of people are beginning to focus on how their strengths, talents and skills can be harnessed to fully meet changing times and priorities. Increasingly people are realising that they cannot wait for companies and governments to get their acts together; they must act individually on their own behalf, while working with others for the benefit of all. This again follows the fundamental principle of to clean up the street, get your own house in order first.

CHANGING STREAMS PORPOISELY

Whether people are engaged in high powered, demanding, routine, repetitive, prestigious, well paid or whatever jobs, they are often secretly frustrated maestros at a specific hobby.

Many spend what little free time they have on practising the skills and talents that come naturally to them, be it with food, people or animals. When it occurs to them that perhaps they could make a living doing what they enjoy most, they too often face self-doubt and the doubts of family, friends and business colleagues, who in turn ask them if they are going through a mid-life crisis, and, if they are, don't worry it'll soon pass.

For those who believe in themselves and persevere, however, the time always comes when they are able to act on their natural inclination. Proper stewardship of your talents and confidence in your skills will always assist you in determining the work that is ideal for you to do away from the fast current or boiling waters. One thing that all the career experts do agree on with regard to career change is that doing what you love and have always dreamed of doing is by far the best indicator of what you will excel at.

'Do what you love and the money will follow,' however, usually gets shot down in flames when it meets the argument of 'how will you live in the meantime?' If what you intend doing for the rest of your life is important to you then it is important to pay the current price for the future benefit.

This principle of course runs contrary to the common practice of enjoy now, pay later. Simply by adapting the immutable principles you are currently undertaking to adhere to in this book, however, will within a time specified by your diligence, provide the wherewithal required.

Both Caroline and Justin Brill loved to sail. Their mutual interests had been the reason for the introduction and the basis of their courtship and marriage. Caroline taught German at a comprehensive school and Justin worked for an insurance company. Most free-week-ends they liked to travel the 30 miles to the new marina at Fishguard and spend the whole time on sailing, working on the boat or talking or crewing. These type of week-ends, however, were not so often as both would have liked, as other commitments seemed to increasingly take precedent.

Caroline and Justin were both fortunate in knowing what they would like to do, but, as both had good positions of employment, making their hobby and love of sailing their work did not occur to them. Justin enjoyed his insurance work but did not enjoy the frequent travelling and the more frequent evening work and was subsequently looking for a way he could reduce this. During the summer holidays Caroline had agreed to taking a couple of her students sailing. Afterwards the students were eager to have more lessons. Justin had also been asked by some of his colleagues about lessons but, as neither he nor Caroline were qualified to instruct he had dismissed the idea. Both were accomplished sailors and the more they talked about the idea of starting their own sailing school, the more the idea appealed to them.

They were not immediately ready for either the investment it would require or the drop of assured income from their existing jobs it would mean. Prudently planning around their now established objective, they first both achieved full instructor licences while seeking to save money on a consistent basis. Ensuing week-ends and holidays were increasingly filled with teaching. Caroline included in her teaching curriculum the benefit of teaching foreign language students as well as starting sailing as an alternative games activity at her own school. Justin began to find that he was inundated with enquires from both colleagues and clients.

It was two years before the planned sailing school actually provided a return which allowed both Caroline and Justin to leave their jobs and go full time into the love of their live. Both their previous employers had benefited and continued to benefit from their new venture. What was previously an extracurricular activity for students became regular, and the relationship and team-building activities organised by Justin for his former colleagues and clients proved useful in client building.

"Going into business in a completely different line to what you have been trained to do is like being lost at sea at first,"

said Justin, "but what makes it succeed is focusing on what you were best at in your previous career. For me my greatest strength was being able to guide people towards the future security by clearly showing the benefits of planning their voyage through what was for them uncharted jargon. For Caroline her strength was developing the confidence in her students to speak in a foreign language. Both of us were providing the means how to confidently enter uncharted waters. For us sailing brought it all together and provided us the living we wanted."

Caroline and Justin's story illustrates the importance of planning while capitalising on existing skills and acquiring new ones. A personal hobby is quite often a source of skills, knowledge and experience that can be turned into a career. And often the only thing preventing you from developing those skills and interests is the money, which in turn is unwittingly spent on distractions to take your mind, or escape your body, from having to do what you have previously convinced yourself you should or have to do.

How will you know if an alternative career is going to be right for you? How will you know if you can or will be a success at it? You will know when all your enthusiasm, determination and persistence manifests itself into a ferocity unlike anything else in your life. For it is the ferociousness that will ultimately carry you through the most difficult times when your resolve is tested to the full and everyone and everything is urging you to come back to a safe harbour. That kind of ferocity is prevalent in everyone, although usually it is fully absorbed into keeping the head just above the boiling waters of consumer demand, rather than keeping the head focused in the calmer waters of simpler living.

People who love their work will tell you it is an extension of themselves, an instinctual obsession. If they don't yet have the formal training or the necessary experience, they are driven to get it. And people who love their work are really good at it become naturally best at what they do. Channel your ferocity of strengths and natural ability to work for you not against you. In this way the river less travelled becomes the only river to travel.

9 Fishing In The Pool of Opportunity

There is no security in life, only opportunity.
Mark Twain

BEFORE CLEARING OUT YOUR WARDROBES or cupboards, you first had to make a bigger mess of the room they were in. Just focusing on the mess would make it appear that, far from simplifying your life, you were actually making it worse. With such a simple task of clearing out a room, of course, you understand and accept any temporary chaos as being part of the process of simplification. When, though, you begin to deal with the significantly more important task of creating a fulfilling life's work, the resulting temporary upheaval can seem overwhelming. If you are unsure, or lose sight of your purpose, you can feel like you are drowning in disorder.

This is especially true when working towards doing what you have decided to do demands major changes in your lifestyle. Just the idea of letting go of a financially secure and regular position or moving to another area, can be very disruptive. When you envisage a change of direction it is usually accompanied by a feeling of unwillingness, and when you are unwilling, you lack the strength of decisive action. The word *crisis* is derived from the Greek *krinein:* to decide. Crisis is what happens when we don't decide. The simplest remedy for every case of frustration and stress is to take decisive action, to address the situation that is the root cause of the disorder.

Whatever it is that you currently do, or plan to do, understand that you are able to dramatically improve your ability by purposely seeking the skills and knowledge you need. Immersing yourself in your heart's desire will literally open, draw, create and develop all the opportunities you need. The key is to be absolutely sure of what is your heart's desire, for if not, it will not be possible to see, let alone recognise, appropriate opportunity even if it's staring you in the face.

LEARNING HOW TO SWIM

All that stands between you and what you are capable of really achieving is taking the decisive action to learn. The majority of people spend a fortune on the outside of their head in the form of hair, mouth and face-care with cosmetics, gels, foams, paste and shampoo, and almost nothing on the inside of their head. The average person will spend £600 a year on care stuff and nothing on self-education. Self-education is the only worthwhile form of education there is and learning is without doubt the primary means for improving self-esteem.

Deciding on engaging in life-long learning, which improves the levels of our confidence and communication, the key factors in our ability to achieve, is somewhat in our hands. The real definition of learning is the process of remembering that which you are interested in. Why would you want to learn something that does not interest you? For a start it takes ten times longer to learn what does not interest you and is only 10 per cent as useful to you as what does interest you.

What interests you is what will always hold your attention and attention is the key to learning. Anything you can do to increase your attention will increase your capacity to learn. When you first learn to swim your intention is to stay afloat and not sink. That level of intention is important for obvious reasons. The point is that whenever you increase your intention, you increase your attention, and with it, your ability to learn.

Only a clear purpose will automatically increase your intention and with it your attention. Even learning the more mundane aspects of your subject becomes more interesting when you keep in mind your reason for wanting to learn them. So again it is fundamental to have a purpose for what you want to do or are currently doing.

When you have purpose your love, and subsequent skill and ability, for what you do inevitably grows. When you don't, nothing will grow in the way that is beneficial for you. Something will always grow in its place, of course, but you will not like what it is. And there is a specific purpose for reiterating the point. If you do not establish a firm desire and reason for your future accomplishments you will find it nigh impossible to keep to the sixth promise that is vital to the successful achievement of your financial independence.

THE SIXTH LAW FOR FINANCIAL INDEPENDENCE

Promise yourself that you will continually increase your earning capacity through the self-improvement, study and practice of both your character and competence.

Make this promise in the knowledge that for your life to continually improve, you must continually work at improving yourself. The Sixth Law follows the principle that your own growth is ultimately your own responsibility. Here again, though, this is contrary to the conditioned belief that any expression of self-interest is unhealthy. The fact is that only by pursuing self-interest first, are you able to help others in turn.

Our natural self-interest streak performs an essential service. While exercising your right to pursue economic self-interest, you are fulfilling your duty to society in helping it conquer scarcity. And remember it is the scarcity mentality that is the biggest barrier in preventing balanced growth in both society and the individual. It is the scarcity mentality that has spawned the belief that there will never be enough.

It is important not to misinterpret what is intended here. Self-interest springs from wanting to fulfil a desire. You would not have the desire unless you had the inherent ability for its fulfilment. But for a desire to be worthwhile and fulfilling it must ultimately emanate from the right motives. More often than not people are self interested because of the wrong motives. They may want power and wealth, for example, simply to exert control over others. Their moves towards self-interest are based on right moves only, not right motives. The two must be in concert for self-interest to be the benefit of all.

Self-interest, or personal development, itself is fundamental to our physical, emotional, mental and spiritual growth. Yet under the wrong or misguided motives, its pursuit has become distorted. Consequently society has deemed that all pursuit of it, even if for good intentions, should cause us to feel guilty. Ask yourself: whenever you do something just for yourself, do you feel that you have to explain your actions to another? Do you feel guilty whenever you take the time to cosset or pamper yourself? Are you concerned that others might think you are being selfish whenever you answer 'No' to any invitation to something that does not particularly interest you? And when you do decide to work really hard towards something that interest you, or is relevant to your growth, do you feel hard done by for having to do it?

Our natural inclination is to barter or exchange one thing for another. Further, we will always naturally do what brings us economic gain or help us avoid economic loss. This means working on our own natural resources in order that we can obtain the highest price in the exchange market-place.

The extraneous influences of society and our self-imposed guilt, however, cause us to expend more energy, innovation and creativity getting *out* of doing something than the effort required to actually *do* something. The resulting tendency is to seek to manipulate basic opportunities, events and positions to our advantage, rather than creating and discovering new exciting opportunities that are perfect for us.

Do you openly read self-improvement books? When you speak to another, who is well informed and passionate about their subject, how do you feel? Is it guilty for not being so informed and passionate yourself about something? Do you feel cynical and judgmental towards the other? What often inhibits our own natural desire to learn is judging *ourselves* for not already knowing. When we judge ourselves for not already knowing, we miss the opportunity to learn now.

Once we develop the desire to dramatically improve our character and competence through a process of continuous improvement then our natural propensity to *significantly increase* our capacity to earn will take command.

21 TRIBUTARIES TO INCREASE YOUR EARNING CAPACITY

Your security and greater earning capacity go hand in glove. They will in future depend on your employer-mindset, your employability, and your resilience. The importance of having an employer mentality has already been recommended. It is your abilities, expertise, specialist skills and attitudes that will increase the attractiveness of your employability towards your employers, clients and customers. And it will be your ability to bend and not break, to let go of the outdated and learn the new, to bounce back quickly from disappointment, to live with high levels of uncertainty with flexibility that must form the basis of our resilience.

To attain your ultimate objective you must develop the full potential of your ultimate asset ~ you. Inclusion of any of the following 21 points into your daily work over the next month will assist you in making some measurable increase in your earning capacity. Remember though you are not into quick-fix results, you are engaged in sustainable attributes.

INVEST IN YOU & CO.

1. Immediately become a life-long student of what you want to do, or currently do. Consider and calculate how many hours a night you watch TV, cut it down by 25 per cent and invest this saved time in study. Call this: 'You & Co.' study time. You are in the business of making You & Co. highly successful. Get a weekly programme guide and select in advance the TV you want to watch. Let yourself be in command of it. It must not take precedence over You & Co.

2. Visit the book shop every month and invest in at least one book that is specific for your subject. Use this as your study guide, reading it every night digesting the ideas. Mark the book with your notes and thoughts.

3. Find out who the leaders are that excel in your chosen field. Read their books, and invest in attending their seminars when possible. They will have already been through what you are now committed to doing so learn from them. Make it your goal to be a real specialist in your subject. If your chosen subject is not what you currently earn money from, then the process of this goal will first confirm your interest and secondly begin to build the confidence to earn from it.

4. Invest 1 per cent of your day on the You & Co. creative department. This involves getting up 14 minutes earlier than your usual time, sitting down at a table with a your note book and writing down any ideas that come to you. Innovation is the key requirement for increased productivity in business today. Rather than looking in the mirror every

morning and thinking 'how can I improve my life', with a big sigh, there is nothing better than crystallising your thoughts on paper. You may choose to do this exercise last thing at night, although mornings seems to have the advantage for the dawning of new ideas. Whatever they are write them down. Also use this time to reconsider how your goals are going. Are you on track? Are you being distracted? Do not use this time to plan your day ~ it is a waste of your creative juices. You will find that after a couple of weeks the ideas and thoughts that come to you will assist your personal motivation, your planning and how you are directing yourself. You may just decide to take the time to sit, think and see what comes to you in this quiet time. The idea is to start utilising your Superconscious (see Chapter 6: 'Learn to Listen': Born To Succeed)

5. Invest the very last 10 minutes of each workday, wherever you are, planning your next day. Make a note of key tasks that you want to attend to. As this list is to be made the very last thing before you leave your work area leave it where you will see it first thing as you start your work day. If an office, then the list is in your diary, if travelling, the list is with your keys, if at home the list is on your work table.

6. Invest at least 1 hour each week on reviewing your personal mission, values and goals. This time will keep your life on track. Ask yourself what steps have I taken that are helping move towards fulfilling my mission and what steps have I allowed myself to take which have distracted me from my chosen path. There is no neutral, you are either moving forward or moving backward. Nature does not allow you to stand still.

7. Invest some of your work time in questioning yourself about every one of the current processes that forms the basis of what you do. You may discover that some processes just go round in a circle without achieving anything at all. In recent years as larger organisations have begun to question and review current practice they have discovered inter-departmental processes that achieve absolutely nothing at all. The system often no longer exists. Taking yourself 'out of the box' and considering alternatives to why you do your work the way you do, could result in significant increases in effectiveness and productivity.

As a child we ask why? As an adult we do not. Does accepting a status quo mean we have stopped growing? Robotically doing something because it works, we're used to it, we were told to do it that way, that's the way it is around here, or don't rock the boat, runs contrary to the spirit of growth. The future is not an extension of the past and what is deemed impossible today will most certainly be possible tomorrow. And what cannot be done will bring fame and fortune once more to the individual who, refusing to hear such cries, takes the time to question why something is done in order to see how it can be done better.

8. Invest the time in your regular evaluation and appraisal of your own work and ability. Why wait to be appraised by employers, colleagues, partners or customers? If you are not certain of your own motives how can you be certain of the motives of others? How often do you appraise, evaluate and judge others? Daily? Is it possible to do so without daily evaluating or judging our own actions? Common-sense tells us it is not though it is common practice to do so. Use this evaluation time to find out what you are good at not what

you are bad at. When you have done this keep working on those strengths you are good at and not the weaknesses you are bad at. In this way your strengths will be able to continue to grow to the point that you will be renowned for them, rather than just put to one side while you can spend all your energy improving a weakness. Why be a 'good all rounder' when you can be a champion in your field? Who wants to be 'a good egg' trapped in the shell of mediocrity. Never seek to eliminate your weaknesses as everyone has thousands of them. Concentrate all of your efforts on your strengths and you will in time be able to manage, delegate or overcome your weaknesses. Don't be a person who concentrates on what can't be done, be someone who only concentrates on what can be done.

9. Invest daily time out. Take time for a lunch break. Take a walk, even if it is just around the office, house, garden, park, street. Don't eat a sandwich at your desk or at the wheel.

Relax, breathe properly, stretch, do something which is not work related. Read a novel, not the paper. Time out saves time off, frustration and stress. Again common sense but can you keep to it for more than a week? Is that your shopping time? Catch up time? Finish report time? If it's a work related lunch don't just talk business. People are people and building relationships is what makes the deal, not solely talking about it. Are your very last words before you die going to be: 'I wish I'd spent more time at the office?'

10. Invest time in your personal development. Read self-help material on confidence and self-esteem building. Listen to motivational and learning tapes in the car rather than the radio. Being a self-starter is the primary factor in You & Co.'s future growth. Even though it may be well meaning, there is so much 'negativity' emanating from so many direct and indirect influences, that you must counter balance its absorption with regular positive and good news listening. Creativity, which is the basis of wealth creation, requires the right input for it to grow. Amazingly, even though belief in yourself and goal setting are the accepted number one factors in success, you will not have been taught them in your formative years. You therefore owe to yourself to make personal growth material an essential part of your mental diet.

YOUR CUSTOMER

11. Understand what a customer is. A customer is the person, client, company, whatever, that ultimately pays you. Consequently your responsibility to their needs and

expectations is absolutely paramount. Whatever you do your job is to serve the customer with your utmost attention. If you have a problem with accepting this, then you have a *big* problem. To a customer you are the company, no matter what your job. It should not make any difference whether you work for an organisation that never sees a customer you still represent You & Co., where you are the Managing Director with a lifetime contract.

12. Do find out who your customer is. The general feeling in business today is sadly one that considers it is the salesperson's job to solely know and deal with the customer. Usually the person who gives the instruction, manages and 'runs' the operation, has never met the customer, even though the customer, not the shareholder, is the one providing the wherewithal. The successes of the next generation of businesses will only be those who are customer-focused. Currently, however, the majority of decision makers have never met their customer. Their working lives are too full of meetings about how to increase productivity to talk to the customer. Yet it is only the customer who has the ability to directly increase their productivity. Don't remove yourself from customer contact.

13. Find out what your customer wants to achieve. A customer is not interested in how good your company or you are, what you have done and where you are going. A customer is only interested in how you can help them succeed and grow. For example, who do you look for first in photographs which include you? Is it your aunt, partner, child, colleague? No, it's you isn't it? There's nothing wrong with that. People are people. So find out what they want,

why they are in business, what their mission is, what their goals and objectives are.

14. Discover how you can best serve your customer. Knowing everything you can about your customer's needs, aspirations and goals will help you in developing innovative and creative ways to best serve their interests. Again, sadly, many view serving others as being servile. This is a severely restricting mind-set to have and if you feel you suffer from it then you must diligently work at changing it. We can only serve ourselves best through serving others first. The I can only be developed through the we.

15. Take the initiative and be proactive. Don't wait to be contacted, receive an order or commission, work at developing proposals that will help your customer to grow stronger. Build your success on their success. During depressions or recessions when redundancy is endemic, the

usual mindset is to prepare CVs (curriculum vitae), send off for job applications and await a response. Some are prepared to do any type of work, some are more selective, but none consider the person or company they are contacting as their customer:

Tom Sprat was distraught at being made redundant for the second time in three years. Having spent so much time in making applications before to no avail he was not too enthusiastic about starting again. He was good at his work and it was only because he had been a recent employee that the rationalisation from his firm's merger had affected him. This time he was determined to be more proactive, more in command of events and to fully utilise his strengths and talents.

The first thing he did was to identify the three main companies that were local to his area where he believed his employment would bring added value. These will be my customers, he decided, and over the next six weeks he fully researched everything he could learn about them. He tried their products, their services, read their accounts, their history, understood their ethos, their mission, their objectives, industry and market place. He contacted a press clipping agency and asked them to provide everything they could about his three 'customers'.

He had visited the office receptions several times on the genuine basis that he wanted to find out more about their products and services. He also took a week to visit all their outlets and speak to people about their service and products. Finding out who the key decision maker was, he then wrote to each company. Here is a copy of a letter he wrote to one of them:

Dear Mr Mackerel,

Impressed with your operation I took it upon myself to understand more about it. During the past two months I have fully researched your company's products and services and visited all of your outlets.

My intention was to discover how to bring added value to an already successful operation. Notwithstanding my 15 years of experience in the industry, I specifically put myself in the shoes of being one of your customers. In this way I was able to consider ideas from an external stance, rather than an internal position.

For the above reason I can in all honesty and enthusiasm write to you in the knowledge of being able to provide added value to you and your company. The opportunity for employment may not currently exist at the moment but I would sincerely request that you consider me when your continued growth requires it.

In the meantime I would be happy to share and discuss my ideas with you should you so wish to do so.
Yours with commitment,

Tom Sprat

Forty-six year old Tom did get a meeting. Why would he not? If you were boss of a company and got a letter saying how he could improve your success, rather than just asking for a job, wouldn't you want to take it further. Isn't that what business is about? Isn't a meeting better than an interview? Isn't an interview better than a rejection letter? If you need or want a different job or position, don't just apply.

Understand everything you can about a company first. Even if you don't use the information you will feel more confident because of it. The rule is that people do not buy companies and they do not buy products. People buy people. People who have an air of conviction and self assured belief about themselves, what they are, do and what they are able to deliver.

Make a habit to continually ask and appraise yourself of: Who your customer is? What are their needs? What are their expectations? What is my product or service? How does it meet their needs and expectations? How can I better serve my customers?

YOUR OPPORTUNITIES

16. Detail exactly what you consider your job responsibility is. This is not your job description, because your work should no longer be what you do, your work should reflect what you are. When you know exactly what your responsibility is you can start to notice opportunities that are in concert with it. For example the common refrain of: 'That's not my job', or 'it's no good asking me', or 'how can I can get out of this', is not conducive to capitalising on opportunity. Use every request of you as an opportunity to bequest your skills.

17. Continue to convert yourself into a business. See yourself as a self-contained economic entity, not as a component part looking for a whole within which you can function. See yourself as surrounded by a market even when

you are on the payroll of an organisation. Keep learning how to best manage You & Co. effectively. Develop your own business plan for what you are involved with. In this way you will develop a new way of seeing the work world. It does not even require that you leave your present job if you don't wish to or have to, although the longer and more successfully you use this approach to do your work, the more dissatisfied you are likely to become with the traditional world of jobs.

18. Do not wait for opportunity to seek you out. Keep your eyes open for when opportunity knocks. This does not mean being an opportunist, as this is based on the scarcity mentality and operates under the belief that for someone to win, another has to lose. And it does not mean waiting at the harbour for your ship to come in. It means being proactive rather than reactive. It means being internally driven, rather than externally influenced. It means consciously working on the process of improving your life so, that when your horizons inevitably expand, your clear focus picks out the new and abundant opportunities available for you.

19. Build relationships at every opportunity and not for opportunity. Remember that in the same way your choice follows a different configuration to consequence, you have greater command over the process of your life than the results you may have in mind. Building relationships for the sole purpose of how they may be useful to you is not conducive to attracting opportunity. Opportunity will spring at you when you are at your least manipulative. Don't push people, let people be pulled along with you because of your belief, integrity and service. This follows the 'chain of

events' and 'each link counts' principle. Try pushing a metal chain and seeing how far you get. Leading one end purposely is infinitely better.

20. Regularly get out of your own box. Consider your best ideas. Have they come to you outside of your work or while at work? The best ideas usually come when you are doing something entirely different. It is important that you fully know your subject but do make certain you take time to look at your work from other perspectives. The spouse's idea for her executive partner has often improved the course of a business, simply because a different perspective is considered.

Always seek to see the wood from the trees in the knowledge that the best opportunities are almost always directly under your feet.

Don't let them wait there just to be capitalised on by a new incoming company who has purposely acquired your business, product, service or market place, because they have noticed it from their perspective.

21. Save, collect and use testimonials for your work, but remember to praise and reward yourself also. Letting testimonials speak for your business is by far the best way to woo new customers. It endorses your approach in the way you serve your existing customers. When you receive acknowledgement from another, particularly from your customer or peer group, you immediately receive a psychological boost in your self-esteem and confidence. The result is that your enthusiasm for what you do is also boosted and opportunity seems to throw itself at you, which is why success breeds success.

What people do not do enough of though, is to praise and reward their own efforts. Being result orientated the common practice is for one to reward oneself *only* when the outcome is how they wanted it to turn out. So, if after weeks or months of work something happens to prevent or delay the outcome you were anticipating, the tendency is to not praise or reward your effort. But you are in command of the process not the result. Mentally beating yourself up for not getting the outcome you hoped for psychologically gives you the opposite of a boost. Your work is what you are about, not where you are at. Feeling all your effort has been wasted is not conducive to success or opportunity. Rewarding yourself regularly for completing the tasks you have set yourself while letting go of the emotional attachment you feel to what the outcome should be, is the key to enjoying greater opportunity.

Study, work, opportunity and success are linked. As loving what you do is the key to getting them to play in harmony, it is important to love what you do until you are doing what you love. Whatever you decide to do with your life, remember that it is your life and as such only you should live it. Don't let others live it for you and don't seek to live your life through the lives of others. Make certain that what you do is important to you and is not just something that fills your days.

Right now where you are and in what you do and regardless of whether you accept the fact, there exist opportunities to increase your earning capacity. It may involve switching careers, or planning a move, but it will certainly involve the way you think, believe and expect things and events should happen. You will have already proved to yourself by now that you can increase your saving capacity. As money saved or earned follows the same principles and disciplines, increasing your earning capacity already falls within your capabilities. It is merely your responsibility to take the same principles and disciplines into work with you.

In antiquity fish studied for their own sake; nowadays fish study for the sake of impressing others.
Confishius

10 Swimming Better With Less Strokes

Money is better than poverty, if only for financial reasons.
Woody Allen

Utopia does not exist and whichever way you look at it, living in the modern world requires money. There is absolutely nothing wrong with this as it provides the most workable and practical medium of exchange available. Money itself is the raw material of refined financial independence. This is a fact yet, as this book has pointed out, the way we process it, is usually fiction. The adult's insensitive comment to the child of: 'You'll never amount to anything' too often becomes the truth when a lifetime of working never leads to earning enough *with* surplus, the basic criteria of being financially independent.

Financial independence, the right by all, sought by all and available to all, is attained by few. Hopefully you are one of the few who have so far promised yourself to spend less than you earn; invest the rest; build the desire to control your expenditure; plan towards owning your own home; grow your savings through sound investment and seek to continually increase your earning capacity. Hopefully you will also be one of the few who have taken action towards simplifying your life by clearing and uncluttering the various weights and ties that hold you back in so many ways. If you are then you will be one of the few who will be able to fully embrace the final and seventh law for financial independence.

You may be one of the not so few who, although stimulated by this book, choose to delay taking action until the first of the month; the beginning of the year; as soon as you have finished an important contract; when you get out of a difficult relationship; when you get the promotion that is due to you; after the Festive Season when you can start concurrently with your planned diet, as soon as you are able to give it your whole attention or, simply, tomorrow. Beware. Tomorrow never comes, but is soon lost in all our yesterdays. Understand that right at this very moment, you are the sum total of everything you have ever thought, planned or done to date in your life. And, in one, two, five and ten year's time you will still be the sum total of everything you have thought done plus the extra one, two, five and ten years in your life in which you have not planned or done.

If you do not make a fundamental change in the way you currently live and continue to do what you have always done, then you will most assuredly end up with what you have always got. Getting by is not the same as getting on with your life. Procrastination means living now, but feeling guilty, worrying about the future and inevitably eking out an existence, with regrets, when it comes to pass. Taking positive and proactive action means living now, excited about the future, and living to the full, with no regrets, when the future becomes now.

The very fact, however, that you have read to this point puts you in the rare bracket of being one of those individuals who is well on the path to financial independence. No doubt your commitment to yourself to simplify your life is already paying off in many ways from a less cramped lifestyle to a more creative disposition. No doubt you are also beginning to experience the enjoyable feelings of being in control of what you do with your money and that sense of freedom that can only result from reducing your debts and outgoings.

You will have found that the very act of your clear-outs were a therapy in themselves. Indeed they offer as a good illustration to the paradoxical truth of: less means more. The long, steady, deep and smooth strokes of the purposeful swimmer are infinitely more effective than the short, frantic, shallow and rough strokes of the urgent swimming. The former expends less energy yet achieves considerably more than the latter who exhaustibly ends up nowhere.

THE SEVENTH LAW FOR FINANCIAL INDEPENDENCE

The whole essence of being financially independent is to have an income that will cover your outgoings, *regardless* of whether you choose to work for money or not. For this to happen your income has not only to be greater than your expenditure but it must also be *independent* of what you would usually have to do to ensure an income. This law involves the following:

Promise yourself that you will plan for a future income that will provide for all your needs.

This promise is to be made in the full knowledge that, in keeping your six previous promises and simplifying your life, your investments will inevitably grow to provide an income that will exceed your outgoings. This follows the paradoxical principle of doing less achieves more as well as the principle of one step at a time provides the mortar for a solid foundation.

Although a promise may precede an action, though, it is vital, when considering the importance of such an action, to have a step by step plan that is *measurable.*

CHARTING YOUR COURSE FOR FINANCIAL INDEPENDENCE

Simply by keeping to your financial integrity through your commitment to the previous six promises you will inevitably and inexorably move towards attaining financial independence. Your promises ensure a 'when' situation, rather than an 'if' situation. The only variable factor under debate, therefore, is when. Knowing that a 'when' is considerably more motivational than an 'if' is still not enough.

Only by having a measurable and visual plan will you enjoy the process required to attain financial independence and be at last able to break the umbilical cord between money and work. Imagine not having to work for money if you don't want to? That means being able to work at whatever you choose to, whenever you want while not having your emotional needs put you under pressure for what you are undertaking. What does this mean? It means that you can be your own person and do things because you want to rather than have to.

Do you currently do what you do solely because of the money? Do you often act differently talking to someone you want something from, rather than someone that you don't? Have you at any time compromised your values, your self-respect, even your beliefs or principles, because the instruction comes from the same source that provided your much needed income?

All these and many more are key factors in linking money to work. Yet when through financial independence, there is no necessity, requirement or demand to do what you don't consider is in line with your values or priorities, this impeding umbilical cord is cut, leaving you free to be in command of yourself. And do you know what happens? Your value to yourself and others goes up! Free to be able to focus on what you are best at you get better at it, are more sought after and earn even more than you anticipated you would. More importantly, however, you are free to share your strength and time in those areas you choose in benefiting others.

As your expenses go down, your income goes up, your debts disappear and your savings increase. You will find yourself doing more for others than you did before instead of just buying your way through life. As money becomes less of a problem in your life you will discover that your creativity previously locked in the constant struggle with your finances will be released for developing your worthwhile dreams in to reality.

That is why it is so important to start right now in charting your course so you can literally plan how long you have to work *for* money, in order that you can clearly see a time when you can choose *not* to work for it. It may be five, ten or more years, but when you can see the promise of where your plans are taking you, it is significantly easier to keep the promises you have made to yourself. When the reason for why you are doing what you are doing is clear to you focus can be maintained.

PETE PIRANHA'S PERSONAL PLANNING WALL CHART

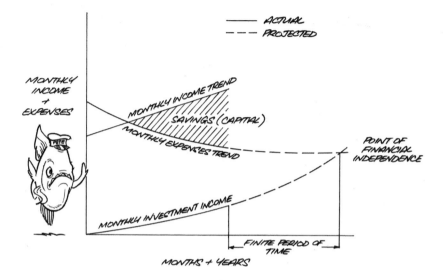

Since he had religiously kept to his promises Pete had a clearer perspective of how he envisaged the next few years. Since investing the time in charting his progress actually onto paper his confidence about and commitment to his word had been considerably easier. And what results! Even in the first few months he had noticed a considerable difference in his spending and saving habits. One of his weaknesses had always been to not bother about his own personal accounts. He had been the world's worst, he had never bothered to keep a note on his spending habits ~ he had just drawn out money whenever he wanted something or used a credit card if he had been unable to draw money out.

Subsequently planning towards a specific goal, however, and one that would fully utilise all of his strengths, it was almost as if his weak points had been carried along with the enthusiasm of it all. He actually enjoyed doing his personal accounts on a monthly basis now. He even kept his receipts for things! It was enjoyable because he no longer viewed doing his finances as a chore, bind or painful experience. No, it was now part of the process where he could actually see his planned goals coming to fruition! Admittedly there had been a few hitches or rather fall-backs in his programme but it was only because of chart-marking that he was able to rectify them.

As soon as he could see that his relapses were literally forcing him off course, he was able to re-commit himself. The worst time was when he first experienced having more surplus income to his outgoing. It was almost as if the extra money had caused him to become complacent, and he was shocked when he saw that within just a short time he had fallen back to his former status quo.

What really excited him though, was that he now could see two incomes on his chart. One from his regular income from his work, and one from his investment income! OK so the investment income wasn't anything to speak of at the moment, but he had not had it before and it was an income which he had control over and could watch grow. He felt as though he had given birth to a fiscal baby and he was determined to nurture its growth with all the right principles, practices and promises.

GET HOOKED ON YOUR OWN CHART

Having your own chart is easy to keep and makes keeping your promises easier. A constant visual and simple reminder of how you are doing with your saving and spending plans not only keeps you on course, but also develops the discipline and essential habits for building personal and financial integrity. A chart is also a whole lot easier than looking at a set of accounts or reports prepared by someone else on an annual basis, which are nigh impossible to understand and make you feel utterly miserable when you look at the bottom line figures.

Develop your chart in such a way as to allow for your monthly expenses and income. Agree with yourself at the end of each month to mark a cross for your ingoings and outgoings. Your ingoings may not fluctuate at all, in which case you are presented with the measurable opportunity to creatively increase it. Your outgoings may quite quickly reduce in the first six months, as the novelty of deciding not to adhere to mindless consumerism is strong. Do try and keep a receipt for everything that you spend your personal money on, in order that you can simply add the figure up at the end of the month and mark a cross where appropriate. It is a good idea to have different coloured pens, using a blue one for income and a red one for the amount spent.

Your first goal is to get the red line of your monthly expenses below that of your blue monthly income line. Assuming that the red line is initially on top, your chart will be indicating that you have to curb your spending. As the red line passes below the blue line the chart indicates that your efforts are proving successful.

The increasing difference between the lowering red line and the static or raising blue line indicates the amount of surplus from your income that you are now able to save. You may understandably think that there is no way that your blue income line will increase, because of the nature of your employment. The fact is, however, that with your mind now free from worrying about debt it will be able to put its power to creating innovative ways to increase your income. Trust in it and it will do so naturally, for it is in everyone's nature to be creative. When weighed down with millstones your mind concentrates on survival, on staying afloat. When released, however, your mind can concentrate on growth.

REACHING A FORD IN YOUR LIFE

As you inevitably begin to see your savings grow it is important to view them not as savings, but as your capital. What is the difference? Savings is money put aside for something you intend spending it on later. Capital is money that works for you and keeps working for you by making more money. Capital produces an income for you from working with your money, in the same way that you produce an income for yourself from working with your skills. The income you receive from your capital is of an entirely different nature, however, than your job income. It comes regardless of whether or not you go to work. As it is a separate form of income it needs to be added to your Wall Chart using a different line. This third line, coloured green, will indicate your growing monthly investment income.

As your growing capital attracts interest, this interest in turn begins to earn more. This is the power of compound interest. Slowly but most assuredly your chart will show your green investment income line creep up towards your red expenses line. Even with your monthly saving being regular the green line will not be straight. It will curve because the compound interest is increasing your monthly investment income.

Notwithstanding that the amount of monthly investment income will be extremely modest at first it will continue to increase while your monthly expenses line remains fairly stable. The important point is that simply by keeping to your word, month by month, your investment income will be increasing.

The time will come when you will inevitably be able to project when your investment income will exceed your monthly expenses. This may be 5 years down the stream, ten or more. It may be sooner or it may be later, but it will be a certain fact, not a 'maybe one day'. Uncannily the day will come when you will have achieved financial independence. And not only that. You will not only have the additional income from your investments but you will have your actual investments, which by now will be substantial!

Your clutter, whims, extravagances and escapisms will have been all channelled into a portfolio of worthwhile assets. You will be an individual of substance, your own person. When your investment income crosses your living expenses you will have reached the *ford* in your stream when you can *afford* to be in a rare position. You will have a secure, regular income for life from a source other than a job.

This realisation can have a powerful impact. If you wish you can decide to intensively work for a chosen, specific and limited period of time in your life, earning the money to develop your financial independence, in order that you attain the freedom to do whatever you want. Untouched your sacrosanct investment income can only continue to grow and all the toys that you craved after before can easily be yours. The fact is, however, you will probably have lost the egotistical desire for them. Your priorities and values will have been honed by the discipline you have acquired in charting a course in line with the more meaningful purpose you have set your sails towards.

It may be that you have a second or even third career inside you. It may be that you have a specific dream to fulfil or it simply may be that you want the genuine security of not having to watch your back right up to retirement and beyond. Whatever your reason you have a choice. You can swim upstream with a specific plan towards financial independence; keep swimming downstream hoping you'll win the lottery, receive an inheritance or windfall; or spend your life continually bobbing your head above and below the surface gasping air whenever you can. The last two choices are very much the same. It is only the first choice which works in the long run. Yes it's upstream at times, but only because you are swimming against the tide of consumerism which seeks to dictate how you should spend your money in order to be one of the herd. When the time comes that your persistence, determination and discipline founded on your promises to live your life differently, inevitably allows you to live differently, and society begrudgingly respects you, you will see that the difficulties you encountered along the course only helped in strengthening you.

GUARD YOUR OWN RESERVOIR

As you start to save the money from that 10 per cent of your income you are no longer spending it is important to open a savings account separate to your usual cheque and debit current account. While building up the habit of spending less and saving, this savings account should preferably be one that keeps your money safe from your hands dipping into it simply because it is there. An account that does not have easy access also pays better interest, than one that caters for your instant access, which is a bonus.

As you watch your savings grow there is another predator, other than yourself, that you have to watch out for. In the same way that your spending money is courted by the suitors of consumerism, your savings will be wooed by numerous courting financial institutions. Just trawl through the newspapers and you will see how many expensive advertisements there are all offering incredible investment deals. Some are excellent and well founded, others are precarious and high risk. For the new saver, telling the difference is almost impossible. All of them, however, are funded from budgets derived from investing other savers' money.

The strategy for the new saver seeking the best returns is usually to go to the experts in the same way you go to a doctor if you have an ailment. Herein lies a difficulty as your first lesson in investing your savings should not be to fall prey to unscrupulous brokers, financial planners and salespeople who want to put you in all manner of investment vehicles that pay them generous commissions. The key is to not rely on experts, because they are not infallible and, although genuine, may have misguided motives. Take the time to at least understand the basics of any plan you are offered. Pay for the advice of an independent specialist as to the best financial vehicles suited to your means and requirement. Their duty will be to you and not some commission based plan.

If the small print says that investment can go down as well as up consider whether you have enough to put some at risk yet. If not continue to build at slower rates until you have more or understand more. Ask what the outgoings are of a plan, what the commissions are, what the benefits are, what the dangers are. After all it's your money and they need you more than you need them ~ you are their client! The rule is if in doubt, don't take it out. Guard your own reservoir, it's filled with the blood and sweat of your life's energy. Don't be a statistic.

RESERVOIRS TO WORK AND PLAY

Being financially independent means constructing and maintaining your own reservoirs.

Filled with six months of your savings first, as a cushion in the case of any unforeseen circumstances, your basic reservoir feeds into your long-term income producing investment main reservoir.

This main reservoir will always ensure that the capital that has produced the investment income indicated by the green line on your Wall Chart, is invested in the safest long-term interest bearing vehicle possible. In maintaining financial independence some basic criteria with regard to your capital must be applied. First, your capital and the income it produces must be absolutely safe and produce income.

Secondly, it must be available at a notice to suit you without hidden charges, unnecessary commissions, special expenses or redemption fees. And thirdly, it must produce, and continue to produce regular known income without any further involvement or expense on your part. Never use your hard earned capital to speculate or gamble in some get rich quick scheme.

When you have either attained financial independence successfully, or, if you choose to, concurrently, you can build a reservoir for playing. This can be filled with either a specific percentage of your savings or from unexpected bonuses or windfalls. This reservoir can be used to play in the financial markets if you have a desire to and understanding of it so long as this play reservoir is never fed from your main income producing reservoir. It should be filled with money that you are prepared to lose, as ultimately you have no control over those markets.

WHAT THEY DIDN'T TEACH YOU IN THE SCHOOLS

Whatever the state of your current finances is down to you. However complicated you have made your life is down to you. Any strained relationships that you continue to permit in your life are down to you. Life is your teacher. It provides the questions to your life and you in turn deliver the answers. Answers which you have to live by. And the question life will increasingly ask of you will be: 'What is it time for you to say good-bye to?' Are you ready to answer? Conditioned to do so for our own protection, we extrude our identities like shellfish. In time, though, our protective shell begins to cramp our natural style. Like some Koi Carp that limits its growth to the size of its tank, believing that is all there is, we too restrict our potential because we refuse to acknowledge the opportunities that living in our world continually affords us.

Did our various teachers in our formative years instruct us in how to bite off *more* than we could chew? Were we instructed how to get *on,* rather than just get by? Were we taught not to know our place or speak up even when not spoken to? Were we ever encouraged to give credit because we were regularly praised even for things we did not succeed at? Were we shown that making mistakes was part and parcel of life? Did we grow up believing that there was no need to be embarrassed for learning from something or for not knowing something? Were we taught that we were responsible for our own success and failure?

No, and through no fault of any of our teachers, who were in turn simply acting in a manner that they were instructed. If we were taught these things would we spend as much of our time, and money, as we do in seeking to place blame for the state of our personal and financial affairs? Do we not have to first be able to answer Life's question, in order that we can say hello to a new order in our lives? We have to let go of one shore in order to swim to another and this inevitably means passing through deep water first.

The plain fact is that most of us are simply not prepared to let go of the false and complex attachment we have to what we misguidedly believe is our true security. Amazingly our bodies and minds become accustomed to the temperature of the boiling waters where the only way to get along is to go along with the herd. For those few who do brave the seemingly colder waters of striking out on their own, cutting free the luggage of their life and specifically working towards their planned priorities will inevitably bask in the cleaner, clearer, and calmer waters of true security, stability and simplicity. So, the question is: 'What kind of a fish are you?'

Epilogue

Five years today! Was it really that long? It seemed to Pete that it was only yesterday since he had first wondered if there was something different than just the fast current, the boiling waters, and the mindless consumerism that dominated his life and finances. Well the old adage of 'every fish has its bay' could certainly be applied to him. He had achieved so much since he had decided to take definitive action, he was certain that he had achieved more than the previous ten years yet amazingly he had enjoyed more time with family.

There had been times, though when he had really been worried. But on reflection there had been no grounds for his concerns. He was certain now that it was only because he had been changing his home, lifestyle and working life, major factors for any fish, that had spawned these worries. The reality was that, even though it took a little longer than he had anticipated it would, everything had run according to his plans. The plain fact was that he had curbed his impatience and had sequentially taken one stroke at a time. He had always wanted to set up his own business and now he had! Piranha Pine Associates had steadily built up a loyal clientele all of which enthusiastically recommended his products.

Coming to terms with how they really wanted to live as a family, rather than what others expected of them, had certainly been the catalyst in developing their priorities and values. The knock-on effect on their spending, and subsequent savings, had been remarkable. And it was not as if they had repressed their desires, they had simply channelled them accordingly. But it was the Wall Chart that had made a difference to how they had coped. It had been the key in the whole family working together as a team. Even though there were times he had been sorely tempted to touch some of the spare reservoir they had built, his wife, Patrica, who enjoyed watching the blue line creep towards the now stable red line, had persuaded him to think again. "Look where it sank to the last time we did that," she pointed out. "And look how the green investment income line is still going up anyway." She had been right and just this month their reduced overhead, from living the way they had chosen, was covered by their additional investment income.

The only thing Pete still found it hard to fathom, was that even though they did not have the quantity of stuff they had before, they had maintained their quality and standard of living. And where before he used to long for a well deserved break at the week-end or a holiday to escape from the frenetic pace of the fast current, he now took everything in his stride and was considerably more relaxed.

Occasionally he would still take the free-way. Although he would always choose non-rush hour times. Once, however, he had been caught in the rush hour. Having been away from it what he saw shocked him. Others speeding along the free-way seemed to have their faces locked into a teeth-baring grimace. Yet others looked as though they had been weaned on a pickle. Some looked perplexed at his own smiling face. With a deft flick of his gill he once more flipped away.

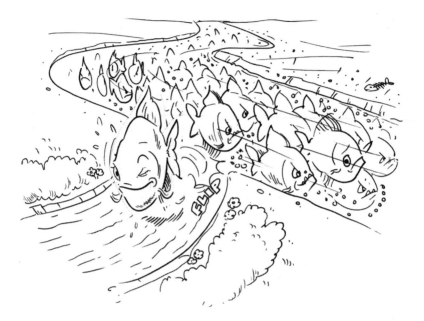

Let your hook be always cast; in the pool where you least expect it, there will be a fish.
Ovid

COLIN TURNER

Passion v Pension

Business today too often illustrates
Man's ability to complicate simplicity

Too many organisations originally founded
on simple entrepreneurial spirit have lost it.

The future is not what it used to be. So why chase a pension when there is no guarantee of one? Far better to chase your passion!

***Passion v Pension* is the definitive guide to Developing Corporate Entrepreneurship**

- Learn the 10 Principles of Entrepreneurial Leadership
- Apply the 10 Practices of Entrepreneurial Leadership
- Sustain Corporate Change with 6 Core Dynamics
- Use the 1% Solution to generate profitable growth

Transform employee-minded managers into entrepreneurial-minded leaders by instilling a sense of *real* ownership.

'Articulates much needed practical and effective concepts essential for future business success'
Roger Leek, Group HR Director, Fujitsu Services, Europe

'The One Percent Solution is the most powerful methodology I've found for creating the sustainable mindset for innovation'
Carol Ballock, M.D., Burston-Marstellar, USA

'Turner Directs with timely advice' *Shingo Miyake, NIKKEI, Japan*

'A source of inspiration – read it!'
Frank Boyd, Head of Creative Dept., BBC

www.21stcenturybooks.uk.com

TURNER

Made for Life

INTERNATIONAL BESTSELLER

One of the classic tales of wisdom
***Made for life* is both profound and extraordinary.**

Delving deep, yet never becoming buried, this self-psychotherapy masterpiece provides simple answers to complex questions...those that *everyone* asks of themselves at quiet reflective times.

'A unique book and most of all it delivers
a very important message. You will love it'
URI GELLER

'I doubt very much whether anyone's life
will remain unchanged after reading it'
HERE'S HEALTH

'A profound, contemplative story'
WAYNE DYER

'If you are looking for answers in your life –
this little book speaks volumes'
STUART WILDE

www.21stcenturybooks.uk.com

T<small>COLIN</small>URNER

The Teachings of Billionaire Yen Tzu
Volumes I & II

"Hooks like a thriller you can't put down!
That a book can succeed in being authoritative about
success, business, lifestyle and spirituality is
impressive. That it's also engrossing, inspiring and
upbeat makes it essential for everyone" *Time Out*

**The Teachings of Yen Tzu shakes the very pillars of modern
thinking and practice. With esoteric secrets, enlightening stories
and insightful wisdom, its provocative lessons present a forgotten
yet powerful alchemy for meaning, purpose and prosperity.**

"As I am convinced the key to long-term success is a
secure philosophical and ethical background, I was delighted
to read this book" *Sir John Harvey-Jones*

A legend tells of a famous Academy founded some 2,500 years ago
by an immensely successful Patriarch, *Yen Tzu,* teaching the secrets
of a paradoxical philosophy that developed self-mastery through
individual inner understanding. Such a level of understanding was
instrumental in *Yen Tzu* becoming Ancient China's first commercial
billionaire; though such success inevitably attracted the attention of
an aspiring Emperor. History records that in the year 213BCE almost
all remnants of this ancient teaching were destroyed by the ruthless
Qin Shi Huang, famous for the army of life-size Terracotta Warriors.
In an attempt to save them from destruction, valuable scrolls were
hidden in hollowed walls, a time-honoured custom utilised over the
ages. History records that the Qin Dynasty lasted only during his
lifetime, a vivid reminder that motives seeking control are always
short-lived. Unwittingly, Qin destroyed the very wisdom that would
have been his greatest strength as a leader. Clearly, the application of
a new thinking and practice is as valid now as it was to prosperity
over two millennia ago.

www.21stcenturybooks.uk.com